Strategy to See

Strategies for Students with Cerebral/Cortical Visual Impairment

Diane Sheline, M.A.Ed.
Teacher of Students with Visual Impairments
Certified Low Vision Therapist
Independent Consultant

4th Edition

Copyright © 2011-2016 by VeriNova, LLC. All rights reserved. Except for the CVI Skills Inventory & Strategies Worksheet and the Forms in Chapter 12, no part of this book may be copied or reproduced in any form or by any means without written permission from the publisher. Requests for permission should be addressed in writing to: strategytosee@gmail.com

The CVI Skills Inventory & Strategies Worksheet and the Forms in Chapter 12 are to be used for educational purposes only.

Disclaimer and/or Legal Notices: The information presented herein represents the view of the author as of the date of publication. The strategies, ideas and suggestions presented have been helpful to the author and are not intended as a substitute for meeting with your local TVI, therapist or physician for guidance in setting up an appropriate learning environment. Because there is ongoing research in the area of Cerebral/Cortical Visual Impairment, strategies to use with this population may change and new methods may prove successful. Updates to this book will be made to reflect these changes, as appropriate.

There has been much discussion about the name of this vision impairment. The term Cortical Visual Impairment has been used, as has Cerebral Visual Impairment. In an effort to reach as many readers as possible, the title of this book has been updated to Cerebral/Cortical Visual Impairment (C/CVI), but throughout the book the term Cortical Visual Impairment (CVI) shall be used, as it was in earlier editions.

Please note that many websites and products are mentioned throughout this book and while great effort was made to provide accurate information at the time of printing, names and availability of products and addresses are constantly changing. The author cannot guarantee the accuracy of this information.

Published by VeriNova, LLC

Dedication

This book is dedicated to my family, Hans, Eric, Ashley, Mara, Evan, Katelyn and Lauren. Lauren did an exceptional job helping with my filming process and photo work in the book. Katelyn cheerfully helped with multiple revisions of the CVI Skills Inventory & Strategies Worksheet. Evan was my go-to guy for all things techie. Ashley was an inspiration for me as she tackled her job as a second grade teacher, going the extra mile for her students. Eric encouraged me again and again with his simple advice, "Just write it down mom and everything else will fall into place." Eric and Ash also helped with proof reading and editing. Finally, my husband Hans, who always encouraged me to do the things that I love to do, then figure out how to make it my profession.

Acknowledgements

I need to first and most importantly acknowledge the many parents of all of the young children and students I have worked with. I have often said that completing a thorough parent interview is critical when assessing and evaluating students with Cortical Visual Impairment. Parents can tell you what helps and what hinders their child. They offer advice on objects and materials to use that elicit the best visual response and many times they develop very creative means to encourage looking behavior. Parents of my students have generously shared their ideas and suggestions, many of which are offered in this book for you to try as well. Parents have not only given me advice for materials and interventions to use, but they have also allowed me to film their children in order to train other teachers in the field. For this assistance and support I am in their debt.

I want to acknowledge the many teachers and other professionals in the field of education who have either contributed ideas or given advice. Gloria Vaughn developed the idea of a CVI Den and we tried various renditions until we came up with the best for our students. Nancy Gallagher encouraged me to cut back on my many varied duties in order to get this book finished! Nancy was also extremely helpful with her editing skills and advice. Sara Kitchen and others at the Texas School for the Blind and Visually Impaired gave me advice and encouragement with regard to the CVI Skills Inventory & Strategies Worksheet.

A special thanks goes out to several people including; my sister-in-law, Dr. Yvette Sheline, who helped to edit the chapter on *CVI and the Brain*, my dear, long time best friend Loretta Hester, who was inspirational and never failed in her support and belief in me succeeding and Denise DiNovi, who always set an example for me and encouraged me with Carnegie's words, "Inaction breeds doubt and fear. Action breeds confidence and courage. If you want to conquer fear, do not sit home and think about it. Go out and get busy." *(Dale Carnegie)*

Finally, I would like to acknowledge Dr. Phil Hatlen, who in 1979 was a Professor of Special Education at San Francisco State University, coordinating the program to prepare teachers of students with visual impairments. At that time, Dr. Hatlen taught many of my classes as I worked my way through the Master's program. As I look back over the inspirational leaders who have helped to shape me as the teacher I am today, I would have to give much credit to Dr. Hatlen. His dedication to his profession inspired me then as it still does today. With his recent passing, he will be greatly missed.

Table of Contents

Chapter 1 – Introduction 7
Chapter 2 – Parents Perspective 9
Chapter 3 – CVI and the Brain 22
Chapter 4 – Overview of the CVI Strategy Areas 27
Chapter 5 – Level 1 CVI Strategies 35
    General Considerations – Level 1 35
    Environmental and Sensory Input – Level 1 36
    Near/Middle/Distance Viewing – Level 1 38
    Visual Target – Level 1 39
    Spatial Window of Visual Attention or Visual Array – Level 1 40
    Contrast – Level 1 40
    Preferred Visual Field – Level 1 41
    Lighting – Level 1 41
    Familiarity – Level 1 42
Chapter 6 – Level 2 CVI Strategies 46
    General Considerations – Level 2 46
    Environmental and Sensory Input – Level 2 47
    Near/Middle/Distance Viewing – Level 2 48
    Visual Target – Level 2 49
    Spatial Window of Visual Attention or Visual Array – Level 2 52
    Contrast – Level 2 52
    Preferred Visual Field – Level 2 53
    Lighting – Level 2 53
    Familiarity – Level 2 54
Chapter 7 – Level 3 CVI Strategies 56
    General Considerations – Level 3 56
    Environmental and Sensory Input – Level 3 57
    Near/Middle/Distance Viewing – Level 3 58
    Visual Target – Level 3 60
    Spatial Window of Visual Attention or Visual Array – Level 3 61

- Contrast – Level 3 62
- Preferred Visual Field – Level 3 63
- Lighting – Level 3 64
- Familiarity – Level 3 64

Chapter 8 – Additional Areas To Consider 66

Chapter 9 – CVI Skills Inventory & Strategies Worksheet 68
- Blank CVI Skills Inventory & Strategies Worksheet 71
- Sample of Completed CVI Skills Inventory & Strategies Worksheet for a Student who Benefits from Level 1 Strategies 80
- Sample of Completed CVI Skills Inventory & Strategies Worksheet for a Student who Benefits from Level 2 Strategies 90
- Sample of Completed CVI Skills Inventory & Strategies Worksheet for a Student who Benefits from Level 3 Strategies 100

Chapter 10 – The PLAAFP and IEP Goals and Objectives 109

Chapter 11 – Strategies for Improving Literacy Skills in Students with CVI 116

Chapter 12 – Forms 125

Resources 133

References 138

Chapter 1 - Introduction

Cortical Visual Impairment or Cerebral Visual Impairment (CVI) and optic neuropathy are considered the most common causes of visual impairment in children in developed countries (Dutton et al 2010). Parents, teachers, and many other dedicated "action heroes" who are involved in the raising and education of children with CVI are learning more and more about this special population as new teaching strategies are explored.

Strategy to See has been written for parents, caretakers, Certified Teachers of Students with Visual Impairments, Orientation and Mobility Instructors, Physical Therapists, Occupational Therapists, Speech Therapists, and the many other educators who touch the lives of students with CVI. It is hoped that ophthalmologists, optometrists and Low Vision Specialists will also find the Strategies helpful to them as they evaluate students with this diagnosis. In this book, there are a wide variety of strategies and techniques that this author has found useful to use with students ranging in age from birth to 22 who have a diagnosis of Cortical Visual Impairment or who have some kind of brain damage related vision loss.

The ideas and interventions presented in this book are intended to encourage students with CVI to use their vision more efficiently and consistently. The strategies are broken down into 8 CVI Strategy Areas. For each Strategy Area, there are 3 levels of strategies. These 3 levels of strategies correlate loosely with the visual functioning phases of The CVI Range described by Dr. Christine Roman-Lantzy in her book, *Cortical Visual Impairment – An Approach to Assessment and Intervention*. In other words, a child who is visually functioning in Phase I on The CVI Range might benefit from the Level 1 CVI Strategies in this book. The reader should note that whenever the terms Phase I, Phase II or Phase III are used, it is in reference to the visual functioning phases described in the book, *Cortical Visual Impairment – An Approach to Assessment and Intervention.*

The suggestions and interventions discussed in this book are mostly strategies I have used while working with students with CVI. Most of the strategies have worked well, however, each was designed for a particular student. Since every student with CVI has very individual and unique needs, the hope is that these suggestions will give you ideas to create your own unique modifications for your specific student.

It should be noted that a student might benefit from strategies from more than one level, depending on the task they are working on. For example, a student using Level 1 CVI Strategies in the CVI Strategy Area of Environmental/Sensory Input, may benefit from Level 2 CVI Strategies in the CVI Strategy Area, Preferred Visual Field.

This book and the Strategies Worksheet are intended to help teachers, parents and others determine appropriate strategies and modifications for all daily routines, functional goals and academic goals in the home and educational setting. The worksheet can also be used to help *develop* goals and objectives. The Strategies Worksheet is just that, a worksheet; it is not an assessment, nor is it an evaluation.

A word of caution is also needed. The strategies suggested in this book include many unconventional "toys", objects and materials to use with students. Most of these objects and materials are NOT child safe. **Teachers, caretakers and parents need to monitor students at all times when these suggested materials are used.** Using a red mylar pom pom may help a student visually locate the target and encourage grasping, but once grasped (which in many cases is wonderful), the student may want to pull it and then put it in his mouth, which would not be safe. Use these materials carefully and at your own risk. Opinions and strategy suggestions found within this book are opinions of the author and strategies, which have been helpful to specific students; they may not necessarily work for every student.

Please note that many names used throughout this book may have been changed to protect privacy.

Finally, please understand that this book is a work in progress. I continue to add strategies and techniques as I find more that work with this population. As I work with more parents I will add their comments and thoughts as well. Please feel free to share your comments and suggestions at the strategytosee website. Additional information about this book will also be posted at my website.

Chapter 2 - Parents' Perspective

One of the greatest resources I have had over the years while working with students with Cortical Visual Impairment has been the parents and caretakers of students. They have been generous and shared not only their children, but also strategies, techniques and materials they have found helpful in encouraging their children to use their vision more efficiently. While writing this book, I asked parents to share their thoughts and views on what has worked and what teachers should consider as they work with students.

KATE

Kate is a sweet 2 year old that has a history of premature birth, in-utero stroke and intraventricular hemorrhage (IVH), grade 4. She also has a history of seizures, but this is currently under control with medications. Her ophthalmologist notes that the primary cause of vision loss is due to, "Cortical Visual Defect, Exotropia and Bilateral Optic Nerve Hypoplasia". Kate is currently working on building visual behaviors and is visually functioning at 3 to 4 on the CVI Range.

Kate's mother noted that the top 3 strategies she found to work best to encourage Kate to use consistent, efficient looking behavior include the following;

"Eliminate all competing auditory input when Kate is using her vision."

"Use Kate's favorite lighted toy, called a puzzle lamp, which comes with a remote control and a special light bulb. Using the remote, the lamp can be turned red, blue, yellow, green, orange, purple, or white."

Kate's parents have found that using 2 arm immobilizers is especially important when they want to work on Kate's vision, especially when it involves looking at an object that is further away. The arm immobilizers keep Kate's fingers out of her mouth so that she is concentrating on her vision and what she is looking at, not her fingers (the oral sensory input). Kate's parents also have a chewy necklace that Kate wears. This provides some limited oral stimulation but still allows her to focus on her vision.

Kate's mother noted the following, with regard to the best advice she had been given on Cortical Visual Impairment and/or strategies to use to encourage use of vision;

"The best advice I have been given is to look for ways to incorporate Kate's (use of) vision into her daily routine. Things such as placing Kate on a black sheet with black backgrounds up when she is playing, wearing red light up glasses when we change her diaper (to encourage her to look at our faces), etc. It was also really helpful for me to understand the importance of a clutter free black background and the importance of using a light to shine on the toys or object we want Kate to look at. We now have a desk lamp that is attached to a camera tripod that spotlights toys for Kate. This allows my hands to be free. Our occupational therapist created a way for us to Velcro a dowel rod across a black trifold board that came from APHB. We have been able to sit Kate up in front of this black background with the light behind us to spotlight these toys for her, we have found that items such as garland, beads, Christmas bells and other single colored items are easy for Kate to find using her vision and a great opportunity for her to work on reaching.

I would also recommend taking advantage of social network groups such as thinking outside the light box that is on Facebook. It is a group that is made up of parents, vision teachers, occupational therapists, physical therapists and other professionals that work with children that have CVI. It has all kinds of great resources on it. There are parents with children of all ages and all ranges of CVI and it is very practical and informative. Parents are able to discuss practical things such as how to make your backyard CVI friendly. Through this page I am learning of toys, and equipment that other families have found helpful for their child that I did not know existed. As a parent it is encouraging to be able to meet other parents that have children with CVI and to see things that they have found helpful for their child."

When asked what advice she would give Teachers of Students with Visual Impairments (as well as others in the field of education working with students with CVI) regarding how best to help a child with Cortical Visual Impairment, Kate's mother noted the following;

"Never give up on a child. Students with CVI have so much opportunity for vision improvement. Through daily opportunities of using their vision in whatever that child's daily routine may look like you are able to help that child build connections and improve his or her vision. Make sure that you are giving a child enough time to see the object and respond, and that the environment is as sound free as possible, and that you are using toys that child is familiar with."

Aslan

Aslan is an active 4 year old in a special needs pre-kindergarten setting. He has a medical history of infantile spasms and neurological issues including a thin corpus callosum, delayed myelination, polymicrogyria and periventricular grey matter heterotopia. His ophthalmologist notes Cortical Visual Impairment as a diagnosis. Aslan is visually functioning in Phase II on the CVI Range.

Aslan's mother noted that the top 3 strategies she found which work best to encourage Aslan to use consistent, efficient looking behavior include the following:

"We have three black tri-fold poster boards, and try to use them consistently to eliminate competing visual input and reduce complexity. It makes a big difference in his attention and "success rate", even though he can do a lot of the activities without the board, so we tend to forget how important it is and how much he still does need them."

"Know what most motivates him. In our case it is the O-ball and the iPad, e.g., if I turn on the iPad (just to the regular screen with all the apps) and hold it up, he will crawl across the room from up to 15 feet away, happily."

"Give him the time (respect his visual latency) and refrain from wanting to help him do everything. It is amazing to watch him problem solve, incorporating his vision as well."

When asked what the best advice Aslan's mother had been given, with regard to Cortical Visual Impairment and/or strategies to use to encourage use of vision, Aslan's mother reported;

"For earlier CVI phases: Break the day into quadrants and for each quadrant, determine at least one CVI adaptation for a routine activity and use it consistently (e.g., activities like changing diapers, feeding, bath time, waking up in the morning, bedtime)."

When asked what advice she would give Teachers of Students with Visual Impairments (as well as others in the field of education working with students with CVI) regarding how best to help a child with Cortical Visual Impairment, Aslan's mother noted the following points;

- Be observant. Take the time. With each CVI child you work with, PLEASE be their Annie Sullivan. Be enthusiastic (within your own self). CVI is a newer diagnosis. We are the pioneers!
- Learn as much as you can about CVI and do not stop learning; a training course is necessary and helpful, but is not enough. There is no "one resource" that covers it all and the more you can learn about specific strategies / programs used by others, the more ideas you will get and then generate (e.g., get on some blogs, meet quarterly with other CVI teachers / mentors to discuss and share, talk to the parents, talk to their team and involve them in programming).

- Just like a "blind" child may need several hours a week of dedicated support (e.g., to read Braille, to learn what things are), so too do CVI kids, and many have the ability to eventually be literate, to read text. Adjust their support services accordingly so they really DO have that chance.
- Look beyond the Phase 1 adaptations (e.g., color, contrast) as those are just the bare minimum of the support and adaptation that CVI kids need; unfortunately they are the primary focus for most people, even when a child is well into Phase 3, which is not fair or appropriate.
- Incorporate attention to salient features, and discrimination between similarities and differences as early as possible. Design work tasks, daily activities, and modifications with this a goal. This is key to their visual processing and imperative if a child is to progress into Phase 3.
- Be patient. Know that going slow is OK. The child CAN learn and CAN find a way to optimally process vision in their own way; we just have to help them find the access route.
- Utilize targeted variation. Do not be quick to say the child cannot do "X" or that the child is too cognitively impaired; instead:
    - Be relentless in your creativity to figure out how to reach them
    - If something is not "working", try a different method
    - Meet the child where he/she is
    - Do not assume your way or the way it worked with another child, is "the right way"
    - If they learn to do it one way, can you help them learn to do it another way, so they have options vs. just training them to be a one-program machine?
- Do not be forceful; when the child is not engaged, unhappy, or tired, the brain is unavailable to learning / change opportunities.
- Give visual breaks and learn to read the child. E.g., Thirty minutes locked up in a wheelchair, slumped over an iPad to work on three apps is too long for a 3 year old.
- Incorporate independence of movement, as much as possible. It is intricately linked with visual processing.
- HAVE FLEXIBLE GOALS – break it down. "How can I really break this activity down into small pieces (both visually and cognitively) and then help the child learn / build function around *each* piece, one by one, slowly? What are all the processes that take place in my own brain when *I myself* do this activity, but that I just take for granted?". Trust the child's amazing brain to later put all those individual pieces together. e.g., What is involved to learn to scoop food with a spoon (apart from the motor ability)? *HINT: It is NOT hand over/under hand scooping, repeated again… and again…and again.* A few pieces might be:
    - Understand "satisfaction" with respect to food (i.e., which food motivates you enough that you might WANT to put it into your mouth)
    - Recognize a spoon and its association with eating
    - Understand "something" (not necessarily yet, "what exactly") has to happen between the spoon being on the table or in someone's hand and the spoon getting to one's mouth (e.g., this could lead to the moment

when the child realizes he can ask for help, or bring the spoon to his mouth, or press a button,...)
- Recognize a bowl and that it contains the food
- Recognize that the spoon must go to the bowl BEFORE coming to mouth, if the "satisfaction" is to be achieved
- Recognize the difference between a full spoon and an empty soon (visually)
- Recognize the difference between a full spoon and an empty spoon (tactually, e.g., by the change in weight)

When asked about other comments or suggestions regarding use of strategies Aslan's mother might have, she added the following;

"I have heard Dr. Roman say the higher up a child moves on the CVI range, it is often that they need more and more support (not less as many people are inclined to believe). Please consider this as TVIs plan with the rest of the team and as the appropriate degree of support services is considered."

"Similarly, based on what I have seen and heard about in various school systems, children with CVI are often not given as much TVI support time as, for instance, a child learning to read Braille. How can we change this, as they may often need as much time as a Braille reader, and many children with CVI are missing out on full educational and independent living opportunities?"

"Allow the children to move independently! This is so important to their visual and overall development. For instance, if they are younger and can crawl around the classroom (not yet walking or not able to propel themselves in a wheelchair), *let them do so* when playing or when transitioning, and provide the appropriate duration of support (e.g., paraprofessional) to enable this movement to happen safely. If they can walk holding on to something (e.g., a bar or a table but not yet a walker), set up the classroom or their areas of the classroom in a way to enable this."

"Especially in late Phase 2 and early Phase 3, and especially with children with multiple disabilities / developmental delays, the strategies need to focus so much more on salient features, and perception of differences (and similarities) and not only on the more physical characteristics (like color, movement). It is much more difficult to define these later phase strategies and involves a lot of trials before it can be put into steady action, because it is much more unknown and intangible, and really has to be customized for each student. Furthermore, the strategies and activities need to be refined and updated. It is unlikely that a full school year will pass before there are changes needed."

"Also, I think there needs to be much more focused and in-depth training for the teams of those supporting CVI children. One 2- or 4- hour trainings per year is not enough. It may be needed every other month, until everyone is up to speed and is in the mode of consistently bringing suggestions forward to discuss with the TVI regarding adaptations, or goals and activities that would better allow for perception of differences / salient features according to that student's individual needs. Wouldn't that be awesome!"

"Aligned with that, I wish each school district's special needs department would put more focus on CVI and ensure that they either (1) have someone in-house that is their CVI guru (with all the training, support, and real life cases across each CVI Phase to go with it) or (2) that they necessarily utilize a CVI consultant to come in for each of their CVI children and work with the TVIs on strategies for that specific child at least 2 times a semester. From what I have heard from my national network of CVI parents, this does not happen enough and is a very big need. But it is what our children need, and I so hope that we can change our entire approach in schools to better serve this growing population of CVI children. There is much to do."

Andrew

Andrew is an engaging, 21-year-old young man who is visually functioning in Phase II on The CVI Range. He is in a Life Skills program at his local high school and is involved in a vocational class as well. Andrew was born prematurely with complications from lack of oxygen. He has a medical diagnosis of cerebral palsy and has a seizure disorder. With regard to vision, his doctor has noted, "History of Cortical Visual Impairment".

Andrew's mother noted that the top 3 strategies she found which work best to encourage Andrew to use consistent, efficient looking behavior include the following;

"Begin with familiar objects against a high contrast back ground."

"Use fun objects that light up. i.e. light up balloons, fiber optic fibers, lighted gloves."

"Allow technology work for you. We found that the I-Pad has many Apps that can be used for our purpose. Andrew's favorite one is *Free Piano* because he loves to find the metronome. Ours is Verbal Victor because it helped us move away from having to make the books that we started with. Now we just take a picture of what we want to introduce and put in Verbal Victor. We started with one picture the size of the i-pad screen and we have shrunk the size to two pictures per screen which are about 3"x3".
This was great for choice making for a nonverbal child."

When asked what the best advice Andrew's mother had been given, with regard to Cortical Visual Impairment and/or strategies to use to encourage use of vision, Andrew's mother reported;

"That CVI can be improved. I used Diane Sheline's suggestion to check out the existing research on Neuroplasticity to bring scientific proof to the school district that it was possible to teach my then 20-year-old to use his Vision."

"Build a strictly controlled environment devoid of clutter and auditory distraction in the beginning."

"The importance of the frequency of the visual training. We started with 4-5 times a day. Now we do it every chance we get, even in a non- controlled environment."

When asked what advice she would give Teachers of Students with Visual Impairments (as well as others in the field of education working with students with CVI) regarding how best to help a child with Cortical Visual Impairment, Andrew's mother noted the following points;

"The Vision of a child with CVI **CAN** improve."

"Have a goal in mind. What do you want the child to be able to use his vision for first? Our first goal was for him just to be able to see what was right in front of him (a face, a toy, his food etc.) Now, it is for him to be able to use it functionally in his environment and to communicate with an I-Pad."

"Get the child's ARD/IEP team involved in the process that includes the parents and any clinical therapists the child might have outside the school environment. The Diagnostician at our school coined the acronym VET (Visual Efficiency Training) so that all of us could use it when communicating with each other and to include it in Andrews IEPs."

"One thing that has helped us a lot has been the use of a daily data collection sheet. One person collects them from every one doing the VET, we then meet every 6-9 weeks to discuss progress, what is working and what is not. This also helps us notice inconsistencies and we can come together and figure out what is happening."

When asked about other comments or suggestions regarding use of strategies Andrew's mother might have, she added the following;

"Constant and frequent visual exercises along with patience. Adapting the exercises to keep the child's attention and interest at a level where the child is motivated to use his vision."

"Build a strictly controlled environment in the beginning. I believe this was crucial for Andrew's success. In the beginning of the program even the birds chirping outside the covered window would throw him off task."

"Very gradually introduce environmental; noise, light, busy backgrounds. We used a dimmer light in our Vision room and we increased the light at long intervals."

"Know that the child may sometimes refuse to work and step back a little. Always let the child end a session with a success no matter how many attempts are made or even if you have to help a little. Don't forget to celebrate successes!"

Nathan

Nathan is a sweet, 2-year-old little boy who is just beginning to use his vision to reach out towards bright, solid colored targets. He has a significant medical history of SIDS at 7 weeks of age causing hypoxic ischemic brain injury, encephalopathy and a seizure disorder. Nathan is visually functioning in Phase I on The CVI Range.

Nathan's mother noted that the top 3 strategies she found which work best to encourage Nathan to use consistent, efficient looking behavior include the following;

"I felt that a black background has worked best for Nathan to focus in on something. I also focused on what colors he responded best to and tried to only submit one toy at a time. Sometimes a slight auditory cue (rustling of a pompom) helps Nathan know where to look, but low to no volume is best."

When asked what the best advice Nathan's mother had been given, with regard to Cortical Visual Impairment and/or strategies to use to encourage use of vision, Nathan's mother reported;

"Making a black board or putting black curtains around where a child plays to help them focus in on objects and eliminate visual clutter."

"Using bright or shiny utensils to feed them."

"Always bringing the same object out for a certain activity."

When asked what advice she would give Teachers of Students with Visual Impairments (as well as others in the field of education working with students with CVI) regarding how best to help a child with Cortical Visual Impairment, Nathan's mother noted the following points;

"(Use) solid colored toys."

"(Use) black backgrounds."

"(Use) flashlights or light up toys."

"Listen to parents who know their child's favorite colors."

When asked about other comments or suggestions regarding use of strategies Nathan's mother might have, she added the following;

"Don't over buy toys. Stick to few and basics and favorites. IF a child doesn't show interest, get rid of it or put it away. Simplistic is best. The time that is spent working with your child pays off - it's an investment and well worth the time and effort you spend.

Henry

Henry is a sweet, 2-year-old little boy who has a significant medical history of prenatal cerebral vascular accident and hypoxic brain injury. He had seizures right after birth, but has not exhibited any since day two. With regard to his vision, his ophthalmologist initially noted, "Subnormal vision, with high risk that this is cortical in nature given his history of a hypoxic brain injury". Henry is currently visually functioning in Phase III on The CVI Range, however, when he was first evaluated using The CVI Range, he was functioning in Phase I.

Henry's mother noted that the top 3 strategies she found to work best to encourage Henry to use consistent, efficient looking behavior include the following;

"Start as early as possible. Henry started vision therapy around 2-3 months, which we feel was a key factor in his vision improving so drastically."

"We created "dark rooms" in different parts of our home where we allowed very little light so that we could use lighted objects (lit up Christmas ornament, glasses that I wore that lit up, or a basic single light) to have Henry practice his vision tracking. We made sure he was in a comfortable space (on a bed or blanket) and we would slowly move the lit object from one side of his visual field to the other. We only had Henry practice for 10-15 min at a time so as not to overload him too much."

"We also eliminated noise during our sessions so that he would use his vision over any other sense."

Henry's mother noted the following, with regard to the best advice she had been given on Cortical Visual Impairment and/or strategies to use to encourage use of vision;

"The best advice we were given was to not just have therapists and specialists help Henry to use his vision better, but for us to also work with Henry on our own at home several times throughout the day. There was so much we did on our own at home that I feel only compounded the positive effects of what the specialists taught us. Also, reading literature on the subject was a key factor in learning new techniques to help Henry."

When asked what advice she would give Teachers of Students with Visual Impairments (as well as others in the field of education working with students with CVI) regarding how best to help a child with Cortical Visual Impairment, Henry's mother noted the following;

"Play to each child's strengths. From what we have read and witnessed with our own child, each child with Cortical Visual Impairment responds differently to different techniques. Many children prefer one color to another or seem to respond better to certain visual objects/toys. We tried many different objects and then after learning what Henry responded to best we only used those objects. As he got older the objects changed, but we always tried to pick things that he responded to the best. I would also suggest encouraging parents to get involved in therapy and to do their own research as well. We were very fortunate to have a specialist and Vision Therapy Instructor that encouraged our participation and always listened to something we may have learned on our own as well."

Finally, Henry's mother noted that, "Consistency is key. It will seem at times that the process will be never ending and it will feel exhausting, but we truly believe that consistency with whatever strategies you use will give the best results."

Robert

Robert is a happy, 10-year-old little boy who was born at 37 weeks after induced labor. At that time, there was an assumption of complications due to lack of oxygen during birth. Labor lasted 12 hours and Robert was born with the cord around his neck. Before they left the hospital, his mother asked the doctor to look at his eyes. She reported, "He seems to look through me." But the doctor said he was, "fine." Since this was her second child, Robert's mother knew something was different with his eyes.

At about 6 weeks of age, Robert's mother called the doctor's office because his eyes appeared to go, "up and down" over and over. She was told it wasn't anything to worry about because the vision was still developing, but that she could bring him in if she, "really thought she needed to."

At 3 ½ months, Robert was taken to a doctor for a sick visit. When the doctor asked if there was "anything else" at the end of the visit, almost as an afterthought, Robert's mother asked, "Why do his eyes go up and down like that?" The doctor immediately referred Robert to a specialist, even before they had time to drive all the way home. At this point, Robert was identified as a child with a visual impairment.

Many different theories and possible diagnoses were ruled out in the first two years of his life. Robert went to see many doctors and had numerous tests, trying to find definite answers. Robert didn't perfectly fit any textbook case, according to the doctors, but he definitely had a visual impairment that was brain based. At this point, Robert's mother decided that it didn't matter if the specific causes and diagnoses were ever definitely identified. Robert was still her son and she was going to love him and help him achieve to his greatest potential, no matter what.

During his early years, Robert would make progress in only one area at a time. When he was making good progress in motor skills, he was not showing any improvement in language, etc. They would work on something again and again without any noticeable progress, and then one day he would suddenly "get it." Once he did this a couple of times, it was easier for therapists when they knew that the repetition would really pay off, and it would suddenly click, like a light bulb turning on when he got it. At 17 months of age, Robert finally let go of the furniture and took his first step. He had been cruising around the furniture for months, but would never let go, even to reach a couple of inches from the couch to the coffee table. He took his first step on a Tuesday evening, and was then literally running across the room by that Thursday morning.

During these first few years, it was very helpful for Robert's parents to meet with other parents who had children with visual impairments. Seeing that their children were happy and thriving made a big difference for the outlook for the future. Other parents were a great source of knowledge and support, especially for Robert's mother.

When Robert was 5 years old, he was evaluated by a TVI and it was determined that he was visually functioning in Phase II on the CVI Range. Today, at age 10, he is visually functioning in Phase III, Resolving Behavioral Characteristics. Robert is currently in a general education classroom with special education support. His reading is approximately two grade levels below but he is on grade level in the area of mathematics (when given reading assistance).

There have been many strategies that proved helpful to Robert over the years.

During the early years when Robert was provided services from ECI, there were many recommendations of numerous activities that needed to be practiced between visits. Robert's mother had to learn to pick one or two that she could incorporate into their schedule with meaning, and put the others on the list for a later week. She couldn't be a mom and a full time "every service therapist" too. She learned to accept that without feeling guilty.

Robert's parents always encouraged him to use of all of his senses, even when Robert did not seem to respond visually. They decided when he was young that it didn't matter what the doctors said his visual potential was, because they were going to treat him like his potential was limitless.

High contrast between the visual target and the background was required. Use of a variety of textures helped for motivation. Lights and sounds were very motivating.

The best color Robert responded to, as a baby, was primary blue.

During infancy, Robert's mother would put him on a bed, face up, and place her face about 6 inches from him, as she would talk to him. This was done on a regular basis. Finally, Robert looked at her and smiled back at her at 5 months of age. This took months of repetition and lots of wait time before this first response, a smile, occurred.

They found that to identify distance targets, using specific colors or outlining the target with a black, mat "frame" helped a lot.

It was often very difficult for Robert to use his vision with any other competing sensory information occurring at the same time. For example, when Robert was expected to use his vision to locate a target item, but there was competing auditory, visual (side movement), tactual and olfactory information occurring, he would have difficulty.

When sick, tired, cold/hot, hungry, etc. vision was the first to be "turned off". Once turned off, he would use other sensory modalities that were easier for him (for example, hearing).

When first learning to walk, Robert would often stop at color changes on the ground, and cry. One time, when moving from a dark carpet to a light floor, he refused to move from one surface to the other, even though they were horizontally even. Robert's mother realized that to him, it looked like a change in the levels of the floor. He had done the same thing in a parking lot when approaching a thick, yellow parking stripe on the pavement. Robert's mother taught him to use the toe of one foot to tap the surface, to see if it was flat. This worked very well once he got used to it.

Viewing targets in the distance was often difficult for Robert. When at the zoo, Robert's mom would encourage him to use the zoom feature on a camera. They would take a picture of an animal, then she would show it to him on the screen, zooming in up close as needed. Using this method, Robert could hold the camera screen as close as he needed to view the animal that was too far away for him to see in detail.

Now at age 10, Robert is very proficient with CCTV, which allows him to enlarge assignments, look at a Smart Board and look at the clock on wall. He is able to locate visual targets by color, sound, shape and especially when they are familiar. Robert still has difficulty with distance viewing and complexity (complexity on an individual target, complexity within an array and complexity in the sensory environment). He may still walk off a curb or step when there isn't enough contrast for him. He often has difficulty recognizing faces, especially when he is in an unfamiliar environment. He has difficulty with route finding in a crowded environment (i.e. when at a restaurant and going to the restroom and back).

Robert's mother reports that at 10 years of age, Robert continues to amaze her with what he can see at times as well as what he cannot see at other times. She does give a word of caution to other parents and teachers who work with students who have similar functional vision as Robert, "Do not be fooled by how well the student can accommodate for vision difficulties when in familiar environments. It appears that they can see really well with familiar people, familiar items, and in a familiar place.   Then, when you see the student in an unfamiliar environment with unfamiliar people, they once again cannot locate people or objects, without great difficulty."

I hope to add more Parent Perspectives in future editions.

Chapter 3 - CVI and the Brain

One of the most important breakthroughs of modern neuroscience is the discovery of neuroplasticity, which is the brain's ability to change and adapt. "A damaged brain can often reorganize itself so that when one part fails, another can often substitute," notes Dr. Norman Doidge in his book, *The Brain That Changes Itself.* Since plasticity seems to be highest when children are young, it is particularly important to figure out what will encourage children to use their vision more consistently, so that we can encourage a positive influence on how the visual system develops and functions.

Since Cortical Visual Impairment (and Optic Neuropathy) are now considered the most common causes of visual impairment in children in developed countries (Dutton et al, 2010), and to date, there is no "cure" for CVI, it is increasingly important to learn new ways to encourage consistent use of vision and determine appropriate interventions to use when we teach this population. During the 3rd Annual Pediatric Cortical Visual Impairment Society Conference, a tentative definition was developed for Pediatric Cortical Visual Impairment.

"Pediatric Cortical Visual Impairment is a congenital or acquired brain-based visual impairment with onset in childhood, unexplained by an ocular disorder, and associated with unique visual and behavioral characteristics."

Since we know Cortical Visual Impairment is a brain-based disorder, we may be wise to take a look at what neuroscientists have learned about how the brain can get better at it's predictive capacity and what the brain needs in order to make changes. Dr. Michael Merzenich, a leader in the field of Neuroplasticity for nearly 5 decades, has identified 7 Tenets of Neuroplasticity. In looking carefully at these tenets we have clues to help guide our instructional practices as we work with students with brain damage related vision loss.

"Change can occur only when the brain is in the mood: alert, on the ball, ready for action." (Merzenich, 2008)

Making certain that the student is alert and ready to take in information seems obvious. However, often our youngest students come home from the hospital, many on seizure medication, and spend long periods of time sleeping. The brain is not "in the mood" for growth or change when the child is asleep. Teachers coming to work with a child at their home may need to modify their schedule to accommodate the child's sleep schedule. Use of a gentle vibrator or other stimulating action, such as rubbing the arms briskly, often encourages wakefulness. I have often had good success using a vibrating "snake" (see Figure 5.3). Once the child is alert, attentive, with eyes wide open, then strategies can be used.

In Millie Smith's wonderful book that goes along with the APH Sensory Learning Kit, she notes, "a state of alertness is necessary for learning."(Smith, 2005) She encourages educators to complete an Arousal State Profile to determine the amount of time the student is alert throughout the day. By having an understanding of when a child is most alert and what makes the child most alert, we then have a guide as to when and how we can go about instructing the student. Getting the student to an "Active Alert" state is when the best learning occurs (Smith, 2005).

"Change strengthens connections between neurons engaged at the same time. The brain builds on its successes." (Merzenich, 2008)

Throughout the process of encouraging a child to look and use their vision, it should always be kept in mind that providing slight change strengthens connections between neurons. For example, for the infant who is just learning to use their vision, he may visually alert to a red, mylar pom pom with a light shining on it when it is presented in his far left visual field. When he becomes good at alerting to the red pom pom in this position, moving it slightly, making a slight *change*, may help strengthen the visual system.

A child who alerts well and consistently to a yellow feather duster but nothing else also would benefit from a change. If we take another feather duster, pull it apart and use the feathers to create a "koozie" for the child's sippy cup, the child will be encouraged to look and reach for it because of the familiar yellow feathers, but more importantly, the slight change helps to strengthen neural connections.

The student who visually functions in Phase III on the CVI Range may be working on literacy skills. As she is encouraged to look at simple pictures that go with a story, we could slightly change these pictures and ask her to find the changes. A discussion could follow on what the changes were and this too strengthens connections between neurons.

Donald Hebb, a psychologist from McGill University in Montreal explains that, "Neurons that fire together wire together". Dr. Merzenich notes that this helps the brain get better at its predictive capacity. Associations can be made more easily." (Merzenich, 2008)

This tenet might be best explained by blogger Kelly Howell who notes, "You've heard the phrase 'Use it or lose it', 'If at first you don't succeed, try, try again,' 'practice makes perfect,' and 'repetition is the mother of all learning.' These are no longer just expressions; they are neurological facts. Every time you have a new experience, a new synaptic connection forms. The more you use that connection, the stronger it gets. If you stop using the connection, the neurons are pruned away."

Repeated exposure to sound and image makes the connections become stronger.

"Initial changes are just temporary. While the brain *can* learn through impact (a powerful experience), usually it learns through lots of repetition." (Merzenich, 2008)

It will be most important for people interested in the education of children with CVI to remember that initial changes may only be temporary. What is required for permanent change is repetition and slight changes in what is looked at and how the student uses their vision. For the Teacher of Students with Visual Impairments, this may require some creative thinking and the gathering of all team members, as well as parents and caretakers, to discuss a plan. I have found over my many years of working with students with Cortical Visual Impairment that the very best way for the brain to learn through repetition is to incorporate strategies and techniques into daily routines that occur throughout the day. This is one reason I developed the CVI Skills Inventory and Strategies Worksheet, which this book is built around. By observing a student's daily routine throughout the day and noting the areas in which the student is visually having difficulty, you can come up with a variety of strategies and techniques to overcome the obstacles. Once these strategies are shared with the student's entire team, as well as the family or other caretakers, everyone can be working towards encouraging the student to use their vision efficiently throughout the day!

"Brain plasticity is a two-way street; it can change itself in positive or in negative directions." (Merzenich, 2008)

I think of this particular tenet when I walk into a classroom setting and see a student who is flipping their fingers in front of their eyes, while looking towards the overhead lights. By repeating this behavior again and again, plasticity moves in a negative direction. My hope is that by working with students at younger ages using specific strategies, we can encourage more appropriate looking behavior throughout the day, strengthening neural connections in a positive direction.

"Memory is crucial for learning. Where you put your attention is important. Practicing something while distracted won't help the brain change." (Merzenich, 2008)

The CVI Strategy Area that I focus on quite extensively in Chapter 4 is the area of Environmental/Sensory Input. I discuss this area at length because it seems to play such a big role in whether or not the student with CVI uses vision. For students with CVI (particularly students who visually function in Phase I), competing auditory and tactual information is often what the child attends to, while incoming visual information is ignored. For the student with CVI, taking in information through the auditory channel is often where most attention is placed. Therefore, if we want the student to strengthen neural connections that have to do with vision, they need to be *using* their vision! If the door to the classroom squeaks as it opens, most likely the student with CVI will be attending to that squeak, not the visual information that is in front of them. When the boom box is continually on in a classroom for MI/VI students, the brain is creating new synaptic connections (new memories) for music, but unused connections that may process visual information may be dying off. It will be important to consider carefully where the student is placing their attention. Limiting auditory and tactual distractions *when visual learning is taking place* will be a key point brought up throughout this book.

"Motivation is a key factor." (Merzenich, 2008)

When I call to set up an appointment to complete an evaluation on an infant or preschool student who is still at home, I often ask, "When do you serve your child lunch?" This is not because I want a free lunch, but rather because eating is generally a pleasurable event and most children are very motivated by food! I want to observe how they locate their food and what strategies might be helpful in getting the child to use vision while eating. Likewise, when evaluating a student of school age, I observe them during snack and lunchtime for the same reasons. I give many suggestions of strategies which can be used during mealtime (see Chapter 6). Kids are naturally motivated by food and we can use this to our advantage while encouraging them to use their vision.

When applied, I believe the above 7 tenets can help a student with CVI harness the power of brain plasticity.

We are learning more everyday about plasticity and how the brain can get better at its predictive capacity and learn. As we gain a better understanding, the interventions we use will change. I hope to share with you new interventions in future editions of this book, as I learn of them. But at this time, the strategies I will share with you are the best

I currently know of and often do encourage increased visual capabilities, in part, because of plasticity and strengthening of neural pathways. When I learn of something new to do or a different way of doing something, I am reminded of Maya Angleou's beautiful quote;

"Do the best you can until you know better. Then when you know better, do better".

Chapter 4 - Overview of the CVI Strategy Areas

Environmental and Sensory Input

The Strategy Area of Environmental and Sensory Input is possibly the most important area to investigate carefully when working with a student with CVI. This often seems to be the area that is the most difficult to resolve and frequently interferes with the learning process, long after other areas are no longer an issue. Environmental and Sensory Input has to do with competing information that the student needs to process through more than one learning channel including; auditory, tactual, visual, olfactory (smells), and/or vestibular (movement). For the student with CVI, particularly a student who is just beginning to use their vision, multiple sensory input can be confusing, to the point that the child demonstrates signs of overstimulation and/or stress. Signs signaling overstimulation and/or stress might including increased and agitated vocalizations, sleeping frequently or having eyes closed, yawning, hand or leg muscle twitching and/or tension, and a "fading" behavior such as light gazing or appearing to "look straight through you". Other signs signaling overstimulation, particularly in students who are working on resolution of CVI Behavioral Characteristics, is a speeding up of behavior.

> *Several years ago, I was asked to complete a Functional Vision Evaluation with Amy, an 11-month-old little girl with a diagnosis of Cortical Visual Impairment. When I arrived at the home and started interviewing the parents, I asked them if they felt that Amy had any vision. Both parents were doubtful and said that the doctor had told them that Amy was blind. I asked again if there was anything that they might have noticed that might indicate that Amy has vision. Amy's mother mentioned that she thought that one evening, she noticed Amy looking at the brightly lit (but silent) TV, which was turned on in a darkened room. She wasn't certain that Amy was looking at it, but it appeared to her that Amy might have been attending. After interviewing the parents, I began to get out my materials to complete my evaluation. While Amy sat quietly in her high chair and I moved around to set up, I noticed that the TV was turned on (not muted) and the family dog was in the back yard barking and jumping up as it barked, to look in the window at me! It looked as though the dog was on a trampoline and every few seconds, he would come into view through the window. Once I had Amy securely set in her high chair, with a black Invisiboard set up as a contrasting background and the lights dimmed to highlight my lighted visual targets, I began to bring them into Amy's visual field. Not surprisingly, there was no visual response. I then took stock of the sensory input that Amy might be attending to. There was the TV playing a soap opera 10 feet away, bright sunlight coming through the side window, the dog barking non-stop, and the movement of the dog appearing, then*

disappearing, then reappearing again as he jumped to look in through the window. I then asked Amy's mom if she could please turn off the TV and asked Amy's dad to move the dog so that he was no longer barking. I also closed the blinds and rotated Amy's highchair so that her back was to the window. The room was finally quiet and I waited for a few minutes to let the silence sink in. Once again, as quietly as possible, I repeated my process of presenting a lighted target. My target in this situation was a bright yellow slinky, SpotLIGHTed with a bright flashlight, against a solid contrasting background (black Invisiboard). This time Amy clearly alerted to the target. As I silently and slowly moved the target from her outer visual field inward, she followed it visually! Amy's mother was overjoyed and I watched her mouth (silently!) to me the words, "She can see!" and then she began to cry.

In my experience, students with CVI, or brain damage related vision loss, use their auditory learning channel often quite well; use of hearing seems to be easiest for the child to use. When environmental and sensory information, including visual, is presented to the child, they often seem to only focus on the auditory input, or possibly only the auditory and tactual qualities of the input. Again and again when I interview parents of children with brain damage related vision loss, I am told of the many toys the child enjoys playing with. When I ask to see the toys, they are mostly music or noise producing toys. Many of these toys also have light producing qualities, which will be discussed in the section on Light, but most often, it is the auditory quality that the child attends to.

So how do we encourage and strengthen the brain to get better at it's predictive capacity to recognize visual targets and help the visual system to become more functional? For the student just beginning to use their vision, we will want to encourage visual attending behavior by carefully monitoring other forms of competing sensory input including auditory, tactual, vestibular and olfactory. In other words, we can think of it as making the environment as boring as possible, EXCEPT for the visual input. Most children want stimulation, and if nothing is going on except a visual experience, the child usually attempts to use their vision, mostly because there is nothing else to do! When the child's brain perceives a difference in sensations, it is better able to organize itself, the body, and make sense of the world.

We need to keep in mind that increasing tactual, auditory and other sensory experiences will still be very important, especially for the child who is just starting to use vision. However, when <u>visual</u> learning is expected to take place for this child, we will need to monitor, reduce and/or eliminate the other competing sensory and environmental input while the child is trying to use their vision.

For the student who benefits from Level 2 Strategies, there will still need to be a certain amount of control of environmental and sensory input. Children who are beginning to use their vision for more functional purposes are often distracted by auditory or tactual input and end up not using their vision consistently and efficiently because of these distractions. The student who is resolving CVI characteristics is generally *better* able to visually attend while there is competing input, however, auditory interference is often still an issue.

> *During the summer months, I sometimes work with Gina, my student who is working towards resolution of the CVI Behavioral Characteristics. Since during the summer months we are at her familiar home, I felt little need to strictly control the competing sensory input; she was used to the sounds in her home and could usually use her vision consistently during that work time. However, as is the case in south Texas in July, afternoon thunderstorms frequently pop up. While Gina worked on literacy skills, "boom" thunder broke the silence. With every boom of thunder, Gina would jump up, call to her mother, look out the window and become quite distracted. This new sensory "information" agitated Gina and caused her to speed up. While it is hard to control all aspects of incoming sensory information, this example demonstrates that even for a student with a high level of visual functioning, competing sensory input can still be a concern.*

Near/Middle/Distance Viewing

The Strategy Area of Near/Middle/Distance Viewing may be the second most difficult area to resolve, with Environmental/ Sensory Input being the most difficult. Children with CVI often get very close to look at targets. One reason why middle and distance viewing is so challenging for children with brain damage related vision loss is because the further out you look, the more complex the "visual scene". I will discuss more about visual complexity in the CVI Strategy Area of Visual Target, but to give the reader a better idea of this difficulty, imagine moving your face close to a solid colored red ball. Move so close that all you see is the red ball and the plain table it is sitting on. You would see two colors and the image is very simple. However, if you lift your head and move back from the table, then look out across the room with the ball in the foreground, you see not only all of the item directly in front of you (the ball, table) but also the chair, the bookcase, the books on the bookcase, paintings on the wall and on and on. The scene is very complex and visually, is usually very difficult for children with CVI. The further away from the visual target, the more difficulty children with CVI have. It is as if they are looking at a Highlights Hidden Picture, trying to locate the ball in the picture, only the "picture", what they are looking towards in the distance, is huge and with much more "visual clutter". However, it is often the case that the more a child uses his vision, the better he becomes at locating and attending to distance targets.

> *Gina, while working on her literacy skills during the summer, was using an iPad to take photos and create her own original book with an application called Pictello.*

Her book was titled, "My Family", and included a photo of her cat. Because the cat is shy, the only photo Gina could get was of the cat in the shrubbery. Since Gina could not see the cat at a distance of about 15 feet, she needed help aiming the iPad. Although, as noted earlier in this book, Gina demonstrates a high level of visual functioning, she still has difficulty with distance viewing. However, once the photo was taken and because the photo had enough resolution, she was able to zoom in (using the iPad's zoom feature) and see the cat in greater detail.

Visual Target

The visual target itself will be quite important for the student with Cortical Visual Impairment, especially for the student who benefits from Level 1 Strategies. This has to do with the color of the target, the pattern on the target and how "busy" the colors and patterns are. Visual target also refers to pictures, which are often quite difficult to decipher for the student with CVI. Generally, pictures of any kind are not appropriate for students who are just beginning to use their vision. Students just beginning to use their vision need concrete, 3 dimensional targets. Students who are using their vision for more functional purposes may start to make the association between a picture and a real target, but often the picture has to be a real color photograph of that target. I have had very little success using any kind of picture (including many of the popular Boardmaker pictures) other than color photos of real, familiar objects and then only with students who are visually functioning at 6.5/7 or higher on the CVI Range. By the time students are working on resolution of CVI behavioral characteristics, they may be better at identification of pictures, but often the pictures still need to be low in "visual clutter". Simple, color photographs of real items or simple black line drawings often work best at this stage. For the student working on resolution of CVI behavioral characteristics, educational materials such as worksheets and books may need to be modified.

Spatial Window of Visual Attention or Visual Array

For the student with CVI, the Spatial Window of Visual Attention or Visual Array has to do with how many targets are in front of the student, the spacing of the targets and what modifications are needed to be better able to see them.

Andrew, a 21-year-old delightful student with a history of anoxia at birth, CP and CVI, loves to eat Bucky Bites. Bucky Bites are a caramel-like coated snack, found at Buc-ee's, a quick stop gas and food store located around Texas. Andrew's mother reported that he was able to feed himself this snack and I was anxious to observe him during snack time. When a handful of the Bucky Bites were spread out in front of Andrew, he clearly was excited to get at them, reached for them and was able to grasp them. However, he was locating the snack pieces tactually. I decided to adjust the visual array and see if this helped

Andrew. Using an All-In-One board from APH, I adjusted it at about a 45-degree angle on the table in front of Andrew. I then placed 3 of the Bucky Bites, spread out, on the board. Since there is a hard, rough caramel-like coating on the Bucky Bites, they clung to the Velcro compatible board quite well. I then turned the lights lower and SpotLIGHTed the 3 snack pieces with a high-powered flashlight. Andrew then was able to use his vision to locate the snack. Since he loved eating the sweet snack, he was very motivated to look for it and try to grasp it.

Contrast

For the student with CVI, contrast between the target of interest and the background is often crucial. Having a good, contrasting solid colored background creates an "edge" for the target and helps to make the target stand out. Using a solid colored contrasting sheet or cloth behind the target of interest is the best way to make the bright bold target stand out. My favorite items I use to create contrast include a king sized black sheet (easy to wash and keep clean), an All-In-One Board (from APH), an Invisiboard (from APH) and any Velcro compatible fabric or mat (see Figure 5.1). Some mats have a rubber backing (so it is non-slip), a looped fiber on the front so that it is Velcro compatible, and are easy to wash. A fabric mat with a non-slip backing can be draped on an angled surface and stays put. Toys and objects with Velcro on the back can "stick" to its surface.

Preferred Visual Field

Generally, students with Cortical Visual Impairment have a preferred visual field. Students who are just beginning to use their vision often use their vision more efficiently when targets are presented at the far left or far right, at about eye height. Often, they have difficulty alerting to targets presented in their lower visual field.

In his paper titled Cerebral Visual Impairment; Working Within and Around the Limitations of Vision, Dr. Dutton notes that, "The visual pathways which lead from the eyes to the brain, run very close to the water spaces in the brain. In particular, it is the fibres which serve the lower field of vision in both eyes which run over the top of the water spaces and lie closest to them which are most likely to be damaged". Dr. Dutton goes on to note, "Lower visual field defects can be very variable and range from being complete so that none of the ground ahead is visible, to being relatively minor so that only the ground one to two metres ahead is not seen".

Lighting

Light and the student with CVI can be both a positive and a negative. Students who are just beginning to use their vision often demonstrate a non-purposeful staring at light. It sometimes is hard to distract the student or get them to look at another target. But teachers, caretakers and parents can use this attraction to light to get them looking at other lighted targets. SpotLIGHTing targets sometimes achieve this.

The use of **SpotLIGHTing Techniques** should be considered for increasing visual attending behaviors for targets at near and intermediate ranges. This instructional strategy is simple and easy to use, and may help to increase visual attending behavior and the level of participation in activities for students who alert frequently to light. This technique should not be used if your student is sensitive to light and/or has a seizure disorder (that may be triggered by light).

SpotLIGHTing involves the following:

- Use of a high powered flashlight with at least 300 lumens; 1,000 to 1,200 works best (do NOT shine this high powered flashlight into the student's eyes!)
- When a toy, target or other interesting visual item is presented to the student, shine the light onto the object
- Shine the light onto the target from behind the student (over his/her shoulder), so that the student is not turning to locate and look at the light source
- With smaller, high powered flashlights, try moving the flashlight to within inches of the object, illuminating only the object
- Avoid glare reflecting from the target
- Remember to present the SpotLIGHTed target in the student's best field of view (and within 36 inches for the child who benefits from Level 1 Strategies)
- At first, encourage the student to attend briefly to the lighted target (this process may need to be repeated often, in an environment that encourages looking behavior; reduce environmental complexity and as well as auditory and tactual interfering stimulation)
- Next, encourage the student to follow or track the movement of the target
- Finally, encourage the student to become involved in some way with the lighted target. This might include, but is not limited to, reaching out to touch the target, reaching to grasp the target, shaking the target or using it for some functional purpose (grasping a cup to take a drink)
- The end goal is that objects are presented without SpotLIGHTing and the student visually attends equally well, as the same looking behaviors are encouraged

Alternate SpotLIGHTing Technique;

For students working with books and other materials on white paper, try using a high-powered flashlight, SpotLIGHTing an individual letter or target from *behind* the paper. The flashlight illuminates the individual target of interest. Press the lighted end of the flashlight right onto the back of the page. The student looking at it from the other side sees the target of interest illuminated. Don't forget that some students benefit from increased illumination on near educational materials, as from a natural desk light. See the printable handout on SpotLIGHTing in Chapter 12.

Using specific lighted visual targets, especially when students are just beginning to use their vision, often encourages them to look more consistently.

During a parent interview, Andrew's mother noted that her 20-year-old son who is MI/VI had never looked at her face. She noted that he frequently looked at sunlight pouring through the window and liked observing toys and materials that light up. Furthermore, he alerted most frequently to bright colors such as red when presented within his near visual field (within 36 inches). I suggested that she get some red light-up glasses (see Figure 5.2) and use these for a specific routine that she did daily with Andrew. We decided that during toileting routines, she would wear the red light-up glasses. About 6 months later, I ran into Andrew's mom at a conference. As I approached her she started to cry. Of course I thought, "Oh no, what has happened". But quickly I realized she was crying tears of joy. She said that the red light-up glasses worked and now Andrew was looking at her face! She was delighted.

Students who benefit from Level 3 Strategies often find that using a supplementary desk light when working on academic tasks often helps to focus their visual attention. Use of lighted targets is also helpful for mobility purposes.

Familiarity

Familiarity for the student with CVI has to do with how familiar the student needs to be with the target or materials used for viewing. Often, the student with CVI tends to look at targets that they have looked at over and over and disregard new or unfamiliar targets. This happens most often with students who are just beginning to use their vision.

Kate first came to see me when she was 1-year-old. She was only just beginning to use her vision and only occasionally with bright lights and bright green targets. When completing an initial evaluation (including The CVI Range), it was hard to tell if she had Difficulty with Novelty since she used her vision so infrequently. During the next six months, using the strategies suggested, Kate's mother reported that Kate was using her vision more consistently and frequently. Seven months after the initial evaluation, Kate returned for a follow-up evaluation. Prior to coming back for the re-evaluation, I had asked her mother to bring all of the visual targets she was using at home with Kate. When Kate arrived at my office, I tried using many of the lighted, brightly colored targets I have found to work well with students who are just beginning to use their vision. However, Kate showed little response to these targets. Her mother then started using the targets she used at home and only then did Kate start to visually respond. She was even interacting and reaching out for many of these familiar, well-loved visual targets.

This area of Familiarity is most important for the student who is just beginning to use their vision. Once the student starts using their vision well, it becomes less of an issue. But this is an important CVI Strategy Area because if Familiarity is an issue, we need to find out what it is the child visually attends to, then take qualities of that target and "attach" them to other, new targets. For example, if the student is familiar with and enjoys looking at a red mylar-like gift bag, obtain many of these gift bags, cut them up and attach a piece of the material to the next, new target you'd like the student to visually attend to.

Chapter 5 - Level 1 CVI Strategies

General Considerations – Level 1

Students who benefit from Level 1 Strategies are generally just starting to use their vision. They often alert to light (or light sources), single - brightly colored objects, slow moving targets and bright walls. Environmental and sensory competing input often needs to be eliminated (or at least reduced) when the student is trying to use vision. The visual target often needs to be close, within arm's reach and usually the student needs the viewing array limited to one or possibly two, widely spaced targets only.

Students who benefit from Strategies at Level 1 often need high contrast between a single target and its background. They often alert most frequently to targets presented at their far left or far right, at eye height. Rarely do they alert to targets in their lower visual field. Often, they prefer to look at objects and targets that they have looked at over and over again (familiar targets). Visual fatigue is often a problem and many students have difficulty with eye/hand use. Positioning of the student is often important to consider.

At this stage, repetition will be important. Use the same objects and the same process each time to provide familiarity, reduce the latency period, and shorten "warm up" time. Try to have the same individuals working with the child in the same way, again and again. The use of Activity Routines is often beneficial at this stage.

See, "Steps for Incorporating Activity Routines into Your Practice" at the Texas School for the Blind and Visually Impaired website noted in the Resources section of this book.

Use the CVI Skills Inventory & Strategies Worksheet to help you determine the best strategies to use with your student.

Interview the primary caretaker or parent.

If the assessment/evaluation occurs away from home, encourage the caretaker/parent to bring the student's favorite, most viewed targets from home.

Be aware of prescription medications the student takes; some may cause the student to be drowsy and/or have visual side effects.

Watch for signs of visual fatigue, overstimulation and/or stress.

Slow down the presentation of visual objects and targets. Allow the student time to process what is being seen and respond to what is being presented.

> *Gina, a 9-year-old student with a diagnosis of Cortical Visual Impairment, currently visually functions in Phase III on The CVI Range. Although she uses her visual learning channel fairly well, she continues to struggle with multiple and environmental sensory input while using her vision. For Gina, it seemed that unless her environment was strictly controlled for competing sensory input, it actually **over** stimulated her. As Anat Baniel has noted in her book, Kids Beyond Limits, "The problem is that their brains can't organize the stimulation in a meaningful, coherent way."(Baniel 2012) What we (parents and teachers) needed to do for Gina was not only carefully monitor multiple sensory input but also reduce both the speed and intensity of information coming her way. In other words, we often had to slow things down!*

Allow for intermittent break times.

Plan activities for the time of day when the student is alert, ready to learn.

If the student is not alert, ready for action, help to wake him/her up by using voice, tactual stimulation (my favorite is a tubular vibrator or vibrating "snake", see Figure 5.3), etc.

Proper positioning is crucial. Work closely with the student's PT and/or OT to determine the best position for your student to be in.

If your student is starting to become mobile, use lights (or lights shining on objects or mylar objects) to encourage reaching behavior and movement.

Check with the parent or caregiver to see if the student has seizures and if so, inquire about what might set off the seizures.

Check with the parent or caregiver to see if the student have a VP shunt (see caution under near, middle distance viewing).

Environmental and Sensory Input – Level 1

Reduce auditory distractions when visual learning is taking place – turn off the TV, turn off the radio, move away from neighboring students who are very vocal/loud, turn off cell phones, encourage quiet from other adults/caretakers in the room.

A student who uses his/her auditory learning channel quite efficiently, but who has to work very hard to use their vision and make sense of what they are seeing, will often just listen to auditory input rather than work hard to use their vision. For example, it the television is on and a singsong program is playing, it may be that the student with CVI will want to only pay attention to the auditory and ignores or "shuts out" what is presented to him/her visually. If the television is turned off, he/she may then use their visual learning channel more efficiently.

Reduce tactual distractions when visual learning is taking place; resist the temptation to give a rub on the back or a pat on the arm as a "good work" gesture. Care should be taken not to bump into a wheelchair or bed. When there is a need to encourage the student to touch something, use hand-under-hand technique - more information at: "The Language of the Hands: Hand-Under-Hand Technique", at the National Deaf Blind website.

> *Kate, at 1 year, 7 months of age, has found that by sucking on her fingers and hands, she derives a great source of pleasure. So much so that she ignores just about everything else when she is sucking on her fingers. While completing an evaluation with Kate, we found that by gently using a hand under hand technique to keep her hands away from her face, she would then look at brightly lit targets that were presented in front of her. She also began trying to reach out to touch the targets. Once her hand went back to her mouth however, she again discontinued use of vision to focus on the oral input.*

Reduce or eliminate visual distractions that may interfere with visual attending behavior (i.e. sudden movement off to the side). Use a 3 or 4 paneled curtain or screen (see Figure 5.4) or block from distractions by use of positioning techniques (turn the student so they are not facing the visual distractions).

Use a white or black cloth to cover distracting background items. A black king sized sheet works well for this. Keep one in your Functional Vision Evaluation kit.

Walls and bulletin boards should be simple and free from clutter. Use 3 or 4 paneled curtain or room dividers to block busy visual input (see figure 5.4) or cover with a black sheet when visual learning is taking place.

Carpets should be plain (no pattern), preferably in a dark, solid color to provide contrast. Toys and materials often "blend in" on a patterned carpet and the student can't locate them. Use a solid colored mat or a black, Velcro-compatible mat that is washable and has a non-slip backing (see Figure 5.1).

Turn the student away from sunlight streaming through windows or blinds. The student may be visually attracted to this and ignore the visual learning materials in front of them.

Care should be taken that no bright sparkling or flashy jewelry is worn. This might also be distracting, especially if a necklace is moving/swinging.

Teachers or caretaker/parents should wear plain colored clothing, preferably black. Glittery fabrics or sequined clothing will be a visual distracter. TVI's should bring along a black smock in their FVE kit to wear while working with or testing a student.

Eliminate strong smelling odors or harsh perfumes. This includes strong smelling foods cooking in the kitchen, which may cause distractions for some students when working in the home environment. Some perfumes, aftershaves and deodorants are particularly strong smelling and may not only distract a student who is just beginning to use their vision, but also become offensive.

Maintain a comfortable room temperature.

Reduce or eliminate oral distractions such as finger sucking or use of a pacifier.

Near/Middle/Distance Viewing – Level 1

Students who benefit from Level 1 Strategies, generally benefit from all visual targets presented at near or no more than 12 to 36 inches away.

Use of a custom made slant board, reading stand, felt covered tri-fold board or angled dry erase board are helpful in bringing targets into the near visual field (and also creates contrast).

Present visual targets in the preferred, near visual field, usually far left or far right, at eye height.

Often students have difficulty detecting visual targets in their lower visual field – raise targets up to eye height in the near visual field.

A magnetic cover (intended for protection of the iPad) flipped backward and over the All-In-One Board (attaching it to the white magnetic side) allows the iPad to "hang" from the top of the All-In-One Board at a slant. This will allow the student to get close to the iPad*

Caution: Very near viewing of certain tablet models by any student who has a programmable valve setting in their shunt should be avoided. Since external magnetic programming tools can change programmable valve settings by interacting with a magnetic rotor inside the valve, use of certain tablets at close range (less than 3 inches away) is not advised. Discuss the risks and benefits of use of the iPad with the parent or caregiver. Several studies have suggested that exposure to tablet devices, such as an iPad, may alter programmable shunt valve settings.

Gradually increase the distance the student is viewing targets when using their favored toys or objects during play or typical daily routines. Adding movement will help the student visually attend for a longer period of time.

Visual Target – Level 1

Use single colored objects, especially in the colors red or yellow. Sometimes, other bright primary colors including fluorescent colors, work well.

Pair the visual target with movement especially in the peripheral fields; sometimes, movement of the object helps the child to see it better.

Use visual targets with light qualities, either SpotLIGHTed or lighted within (see Figure 5.5).

Use visual targets with reflective qualities (i.e. a mylar pom pom, often best in red or yellow).

Use visual targets that have movement qualities (i.e. slow moving slinky, often best in red or yellow). See Figure 5.7 for a DIY Project using a Slinky and a puck light that works well.

Present one visual target at a time.

In some cases, pairing visual targets with sound will initiate looking behavior (i.e. a brief auditory cue).

In some cases, pairing visual targets with a touch cue will initiate looking behavior.

Use **real** objects whenever possible. When using an Anticipation Calendar, use real objects that the child has had a meaningful experience with (see http://www.tsbvi.edu/Outreach/seehear/archive/Let Me Check My Calendar.htm). For example, use a real cup rather than a picture of a cup. Relate what is being seen to function, whenever possible.

Present real objects against high color contrast (light colored foods against dark plates with a contrasting background color).

Watch for subtle responses to visual targets including; shifts of gaze or body positions, changes in breathing patterns.

Use of color:

- Keep color of common objects consistent until an association is established (if the student is attracted to red, use a red cup during meals; at school and at home)

- Bright, primary colors or fluorescent colors are best; red, yellow, purple and orange often work well
- Encourage looking at faces by creating sharp, contrasting "edges"; use bright red lipstick, red steady light or blinking glasses (see Figure 5.2), or use red, mylar-like material to create a head scarf or wide headband

Observing and discriminating the human face is an area students with CVI often have difficulty with. Researchers have found that newborn infants tend to look at high-contrast borders of objects (University of Michigan, 1970). When looking at the human face, a newborn might look at the hairline or edge of the face. But by 2 months of age, infants are starting to look more at internal features of the face (the eyes and mouth) and by 4 to 5 months of age, they can generally recognize their caregiver's face. Therefore, we could first encourage looking behavior towards high-contrast borders or "edges". If mom or dad has very light hair that blends with their skin color, maybe use of a dark colored headband or head wrap would help. Once the child starts to look at the hairline or edge of the face (the high contrast "edge" or border), accentuate the eyes with light up glasses or mouth with bright red lipstick.

Spatial Window of Visual Attention or Visual Array – Level 1

Students who benefit from Level 1 Strategies, will need to have a very limited array – one or no more than two visual targets at a time. Usually, it is helpful for the target to be brought up into the preferred field of view. Do not present the target flat on the table until you have determined that the student is able to successfully view targets in the lower visual field.

If two visual targets are used, there should be wide separation between the two targets.

Work surface should be free of visual clutter. This includes cell phones (and turn off the ringer so the auditory does not distract the student), car keys and other miscellaneous items.

The work surface behind the target should be a solid contrasting color.

Get your face down where your student's face is to check what they are seeing; make sure there is only one target in their field of view!

Contrast – Level 1

Teacher and caretaker should wear plain colored clothing that creates contrast behind the target being presented.

Wearing a black smock or black apron works well.

Use a black cloth or king size black sheet to cover distracting items in the background. For example, you would want to cover a full bookcase when it is behind a visual target; cover the "visual clutter".

Use a black felt board, APH Invisiboard or APH All-In-One Board when targets need a Velcro compatible background.

Using a white cloth or white sheet will also create contrast for darker targets.

Create a "CVI Den" to reduce visual distractions and create contrast. A CVI Den can be made from a variety of tent like structures including a child's pop up tent lined in black headliner fabric, a Privacy Pop Tent, SensaHut, Doodle Dome; Glow Crazy and adult sized black, tanning pop up tent. Visual targets are then hung from the top and/or placed on the sides of the "den" (see Figures 5.6 and 5.12 for examples).

Do not present objects or materials in front of busy patterns with complex colors.

Preferred Visual Field – Level 1

Present visual targets in the student's preferred visual field – this is often the far left or far right peripheral field (about eye height) for a student who visually functioning in Phase I on The CVI Range.

Students using Level 1 strategies generally do not prefer targets to be presented in their central field of view.

Students using Level 1 strategies often have difficulties when targets are presented in their lower field of view (see Dr. Gordon Dutton's excerpt noted previously).

When students have difficulty detecting targets in their lower visual field, raise targets up by using an All-In-One Board from APH.

The student may turn his/her head to one side or the other when reaching for an object; it appears as if they are looking away from the visual target, but they may be using their peripheral vision.

Lighting – Level 1

Provide additional, supplementary light shining on a target of interest; use flashlights with at least 300 lumens; 1,000 to 1,200 works best (see Figure 5.8).

Use SpotLIGHTing Techniques (noted previously and at the end of this book).

Shine light on the target of interest without attracting student's attention to the light source.

Do not shine a bright light into the eyes of the student, only on the target. Care should be taken when using blinking or flashing lights (this may set off a seizure).

Use of plug-in, natural desk lights work well to shine on targets and workspace (but you are often restricted to the length of the power cord).

Use of an APH Light Box with a Swirly Mat and other lighted toys and targets are often beneficial.

Use of a Philips LightAide has been found to be very motivating for students who have CVI (see Figure 5.9).

Use brightly colored, lighted balls to attract attention. A red 100 Light Holiday Super Sphere (see Figure 5.10) or a colorful Puzzle or Jigsaw light (see Figure 5.5) both work well for the student just learning to use vision.

When using a supplementary light shining on a target to encourage visual attending behavior, dim the overhead lights and reduce natural light coming through windows.

Using black gloves with lighted fingertips (see Figure 5.11) has been an excellent way to encourage looking behavior for the student who is just beginning to use their vision. Use a black colored background (like an Invisiboard) and once the glove is on the hand, slowly wiggle the fingers. Bring it from the far left or far right slowly towards the central field of view. Keep this target within 36 inches of the student's face. Dimming the overhead lights and wearing a long sleeved black smock really makes the lighted fingertips stand out!

Use black, flat spray paint to color a paint mixing stick (free at Home Depot). Then use hot glue to affix a "curtain" of reflective Mardi Gras beads, 12-18 inches in length, in the students preferred color. Present this in front of an APH Light Box or hang on the side of a CVI Den or Noisy Box.

A small number of children with CVI experience photophobia (light sensitivity). Check the student's eye report, ask during the Parent Interview and watch for signs of this. Avoid bright lights, if necessary.

Familiarity – Level 1

Teachers, parents, caretakers and others working with students who are just beginning to use their vision should have a good understanding of the familiar, favored visual targets the student will visually attend to. Completing a thorough Parent Interview will be crucial in gaining a good understanding in this area. Using these favored, familiar visual targets will increase looking behavior and can be used to "warm up" students prior to working with them using other visual targets or before they begin to work on new routines.

> *I was asked to complete a Functional Vision Evaluation on a 3-year-old little boy who had a history of IVH and a visual diagnosis of Cortical Visual Impairment. While completing the Parent Interview, I asked the mother to tell me about the child's favorite, familiar visual targets. The mother reported that there were only a few visual targets her son would look at. I could tell she was reluctant to share with me more about these familiar targets and continued to encourage her to show me the toys or targets. Finally, she did go and get the target, which turned out to be yellow-gold mylar paper gift bag. The mother was reluctant to show me this because it was not really a "toy", but clearly her son loved to look at and reach for this item. I reassured this young boy's mother that this was a fine target and in fact, that she should try to purchase many other gift bags exactly the same as the one her son was familiar with. I explained that with the extra yellow-gold mylar gift bags, we could cut pieces off and attach the pieces to other targets we would like him to visually attend to, such as his snack cup which held bits of food.*

Figure 5.1 – Black, Velcro – compatible fabric

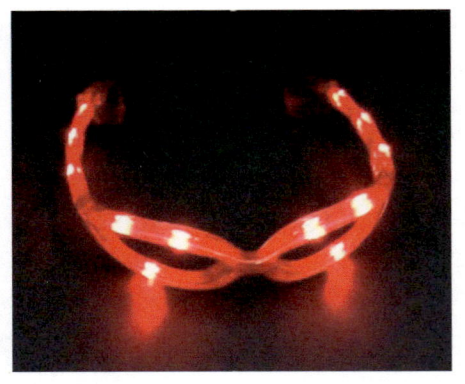

Figure 5.2 – Red light-up sunglasses from www.flashingblinkylights.com

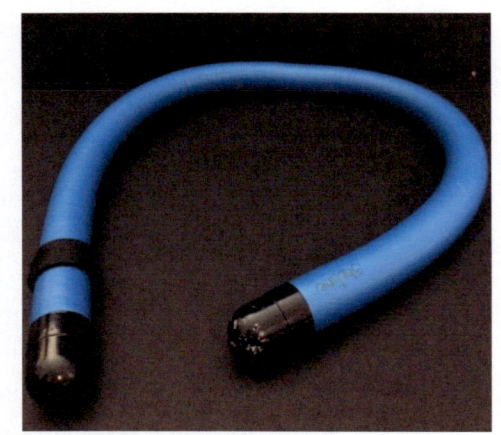

Figure 5.3 – Vibrating "Snake"

Figure 5.4 – Room divider screen

Figure 5.5 – Puzzle Light & Mylar Pom Pom

Figure 5.6 - CVI Den 1 with Hanging Slinky Privacy Pop Tent from www.funandfunction.com

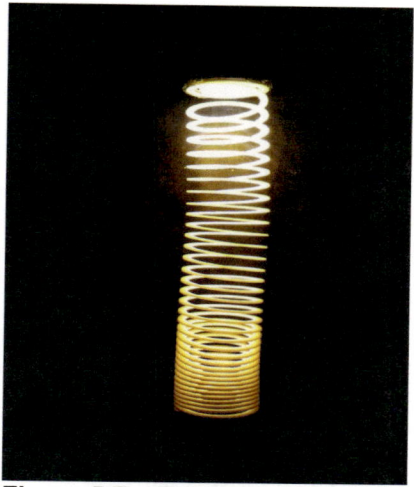

Figure 5.7 – Illuminated spring, see DIY projects at www.strategytosee.com

Figure 5.8 – Flashlight, 300 lumens or greater, pictured is the UltraFire Cree

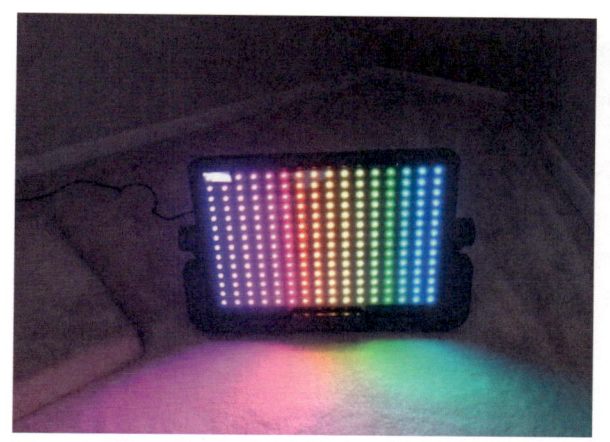

Figure 5.9 – Philips LightAide with Starter Set

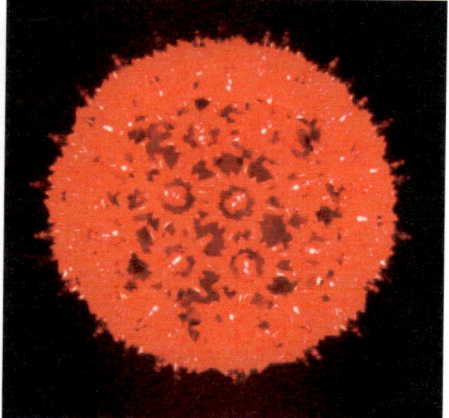

Figure 5.10 – Red 100 Lights Holiday Super Sphere

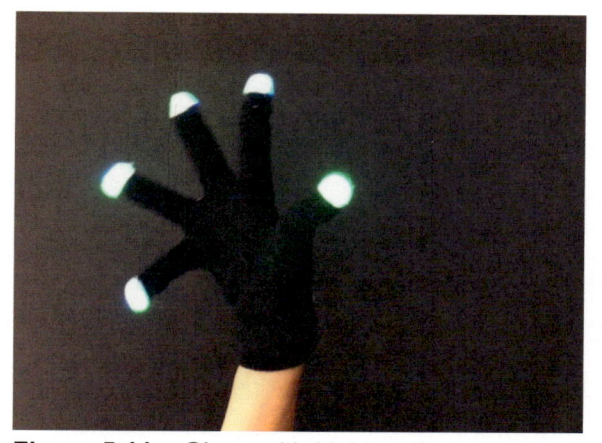

Figure 5.11 – Glove with Lighted Fingertips from www.flashingblinkylights.com

Figure 5.12 – CVI Den 2, Doodle Dome: Glow Crazy, see DIY projects at www.strategytosee.com

Chapter 6 - Level 2 CVI Strategies

General Considerations – Level 2

Students who benefit from Level 2 Strategies are generally using their vision more consistently, but often not efficiently or for a purpose. The parent, caretaker and/or teacher will want to work towards encouraging the student to use their vision during daily routines and activities, such as when eating meals. Students who benefit from Level 2 Strategies often can tolerate low levels of familiar background noise and voices and minor tactual input when using their vision. Targets can sometimes be up to about 4 to 6 feet away, (depending on size of the target, color of the target and contrast behind the target). Students who benefit from Level 2 Strategies can often now attend to several well-spaced targets, possibly in more than one color.

Contrast between target and background for the student who benefits from Level 2 Strategies continues to be important, but generally, the student can tolerate more variety of color and simple patterns at near. They also often attend more frequently when targets are presented not only at far right and far left, but also centrally. Lighting continues to draw the student's visual attention and can often be used to encourage interaction with objects for functional purposes (i.e. sippy cup that lights up). At this stage, it is often helpful to identify some quality of the targets that the student favors and carry that over to enhance Level 2 Strategies. Visual fatigue is often still an issue and positioning needs to be monitored.

Many of the same considerations for a student who benefits from Level 1 Strategies applies to a student using Level 2 Strategies, including;

- Use of Interviews
- Awareness of Rx medications and if they cause any visual side effects
- Awareness of times of day when student is most alert, ready to learn
- Use of tablet technology if the student has a VP shunt

Since students using Level 2 Strategies are working towards using their vision for more functional purposes, it will be important to look closely at the student's daily routines, both at home and at school, to determine appropriate accommodations and modifications.

Consistently verbally note the salient features when discussing visual targets ("The ball is yellow and round"), even though you might not feel that the child understands your description.

Be careful with use of pictures as noted in Chapter 5. Students who benefit from Level 2 Strategies generally still need 3D targets and objects

Providing a routine and structure. Sameness continues to be important.

Observe the student carefully to make sure the presentation of visual targets is not too fast; allow the student time to process what is being seen and to respond to what is being presented.

Use of cues, signals and symbols might be considered at this stage. See "Non-Verbal Communication: Cues, Signals and Symbols" at the Texas School for the Blind and Visually Impaired website noted in the Resources section of this book.

Encourage students to learn through Dr. Lilli Nielsen's Active Learning. See the Active Learning article again at the Texas School for the Blind and Visually Impaired website noted in the Resources section of this book.

Environmental and Sensory Input – Level 2

Reduce auditory distractions; turn off the TV, turn off the radio, move away from neighboring students who are vocal or loud, turn off cell phones, encourage quiet from other adults and caretakers in the room when visual learning is taking place.

When an auditory cue is used or needed to encourage looking behavior (and develop language), keep in mind the following suggestions;

- Clearly explain, in a few simple words, what it is that you want the child to look for and where to look; use "Verbal Cuing" ("The ball is by your foot").
- Use descriptive words about the object or visual situation. Verbally note the salient feature ("Shiny red light").
- Use voice intonation that matches the word or phrase used (for example, "Watch the slinky move up" – raise voice – "and drop down" – lower voice)
- Use an interesting noise or a few words of praise, along with a visual target, to increase looking behavior (crunchy/scratchy noise when you shake a mylar pom pom)
- Try making sound a "reward" for a looking behavior. When possible, try to establish looking behavior first, and then give verbal praise or description.

Reduce tactual distractions when visual learning is taking place;
- Resist the temptation to give a rub on the back or a pat on the arm as a "good work" gesture
- Avoid grabbing a hand to help student touch something
- Move student away from other students who may bump into them

When a tactual cue is needed to encourage looking behavior, keep in mind the following suggestions;
- Touch the object of interest to the child's hand (or other body part) to direct visual attention
- Run the object of interest down the side of the child's arm to his/her hand, to direct visual attention
- Touch a foot with a ball (when playing on the floor) to direct visual attention

Reduce visual distractions when visual learning is taking place;
- Sunlight through the window or light from a lamp may be a distracter
- A moving ceiling fan may be a distracter
- Sudden movements in the peripheral field should be restricted

Work surface should be free of visual clutter, especially bright, shiny objects.

The student may need to move closer to visual targets to reduce environmental competing input as well as auditory distractions, tactual distractions and "visual clutter".

Near/Middle/Distance Viewing – Level 2

Typically, a student who is beginning to use their vision for more functional purposes often begins to extend their visual attention beyond near space and sometimes up to 4 to 6 feet with large and brightly colored targets. Sometimes they are starting to move or become mobile. By using a favored visual object, such as a red mylar pom pom, and placing it just out of reach, the child is encouraged to reach and move forward to retrieve it.

Continue to allow the student to get as close to target as needed; this reduces visual complexity as noted previously.

Continue presenting visual targets in student's preferred visual field, particularly when beginning a new routine or when using an unfamiliar target.

Use of a slant board, reading stand, tri-fold black felt covered board, or All-In-One Board is helpful in bringing the target into visual field. Black spray painted clothes pins with Velcro on one side work well on felt covered slant boards, to hold visual targets in place.

Allow the child to avoid visual gaze, if necessary. Do not try to move the taret to where you think they are looking. The student may turn his head away from target when reaching for it or may observe the target by looking off to one side of the target (eccentric viewing).

Continue to use targets with movement to encourage more distance viewing.

Use visual targets with some favored characteristic; if the child favors red mylar, use red reflective material on targets presented at 4 to 6 feet or outline distant targets with the student's preferred color. For example, using a wide, red reflective ribbon, you could outline learning material on a black slant board at distance.

Use SpotLIGHTing techniques to highlight a target at 4 to 6 feet.

Continue to keep the work surface free of visual clutter (no stick on alphabet strips, name stickers, notebooks, pens, cell phones, etc.).

Use a brightly colored rug or other symbols to highlight a landmark, then gradually withdraw the symbol and just use the landmark. For example, if the water fountain is a landmark for the door to the classroom, outline it with wide, red mylar ribbon, then gradually withdraw this support.

Use a florescent orange traffic safety cone, with a bright light inside and a red light on top, to mark the next location the mobile student needs to get to in a self-contained classroom setting. For example, if the student is at Circle Time but the next activity is at the Fine Motor tables, use the lighted orange cone to designate where the student is to travel to next (see Figure 6.1).

Visual Target – Level 2

Students who benefit from Level 2 Strategies are generally starting to use their vision for functional purposes, therefore, taking a close look at eating and grooming routines will be important. Since eating is such a motivating activity, eating utensils, foods, cups, and plates all need to be made "CVI Friendly", so that the student uses his vision to locate, reach for and grasp the item, food or drink.

Use cutlery that is either a single, bright color (see Figure 6.2) or cutlery that lights up (see Figure 6.3). www.flashingblinkylights has some of these items or you can modify a *Munchkin Easy Squeezy Spoon* to hold a small flashlight (again see Figure 6.3).

Create a "Koozie" made out of red (or any other preferred bright color) mylar-like fabric, and place it around an infant bottle or sippy cup (see Figure 6.4). This can be SpotLIGHTed with a high powered flashlight if needed.

Create a "Koozie" made out of red (or any other preferred bright color) mylar-like fabric, and place it around snack containers, such as Gerber Graduates Puffs, and encourage reaching/grasping behavior (see Figure 6.4). This can also be spotLIGHTed.

Use glittery, sequined stretchy headbands to wrap around bottles, cups, toys or even a wrist or ankle, which then creates a reflective band that can be SpotLIGHTed (see Figure 6.4).

Use toothbrushes that have a blinking light feature, such as the yellow Firefly Lightup Timer Toothbrush (www.firefly.us.com). Remember to clear the clutter in the bathroom, leaving only the blinking toothbrush presented against a contrasting color, to encourage reaching and grasping behavior.

Use brightly colored bowls and plates presented against a black or contrasting colored placemat (see Figure 6.5). Present finger foods in a brightly colored Nuby Easy Go Suction Bowl with the suction base attached to the white side of an All-In-One Board presented at a slight angle in the student's best field of view.

Use a lighted red or brightly colored cup (Walgrens; seasonal item) or use a blinking, lighted cup, available at www.flashingblinkylights.com (see Figure 6.6).

Choose combs and brushes in a bright, solid color and present them against a black towel or contrasting color. Remember to clear the clutter in the bathroom!

Use single colored recording switches for communication ("yes/no" and "more"), one or no more than two at a time (see Figure 6.7). These work well in conjunction with the application for an iPad called, "Answers: Yes No" (by Simplified Touch).

Use common objects in a bright, preferred color, or possibly 2 or 3 colors with 1 of the colors being a preferred color.

Use reflective/shiny material applied to common objects used daily, to help direct visual attention. Red, reflective Contac paper, reflective red wide ribbon, yellow glittery paper and yellow/gold reflective gift bag paper all work well to achieve this.

Use an Anticipation Calendar with familiar objects. Anticipation Calendars are discussed at the TSBVI website, which is noted in the Resources section of this book. (see: http://www.tsbvi.edu/Outreach/seehear/archive/LetMeCheckMyCalendar.htm

Spacing of visual targets will be important, when more than one target is used (see Spatial Window of Visual Attention or Visual Array). Limit the number of targets presented (one or two at a time is best).

Use of Routines and keeping information simple, constant and predictable will continue to be important. For more on Activity Routines go to www.tsbvi.edu and search for, "Getting Started with Activity Routines".

Providing good color contrast will continue to be important. Use a solid colored background, which helps to make the target really stand out, and continue to avoid backgrounds with patterns.

Present finger foods against a solid colored background, such as a bright red Neat Solutions Sili-Stick tray or table cover.

> *Several years ago I was asked to complete a Functional Vision Evaluation on a 4-year-old little boy who had a diagnosis of CVI secondary to anoxia at birth. I showed up at the home during lunchtime, as I often obtain very good observations of use of vision while the child is eating. While Charlie ate his lunch, I noted observations and interviewed his mother. Charlie seemed to locate his food well when there was only about 4 small bits of food on his tray. The tray was light tan in color and the food stood out quite well, as it was a darker color. When I commented that Charlie seemed to use his vision well when locating and picking up his food, his mother noted, "He has good days and he has bad days and when he has a bad day, he can't locate a single bite". I asked her to tell me about the days when Charlie has difficulty locating his food and she told me about lunchtime at a restaurant just a few days prior to my evaluation. I asked her to describe the restaurant in detail including lighting, noise level and how Charlie was sitting. I asked about the foods she used and the tray on the high chair. I found out that Charlie was scooted up to the table in one of the common stacking wooden high chairs often found in restaurants, which had no tray. Because Charlie's mother was worried about germs in the public restaurant, she pulled out one of her handy brightly colored, busy patterned disposable placemats and placed that on the table first, then placed the food on top of it. She further described the restaurant as noisy, lots of people moving around and the table being lit by a pierced metal chandelier, which caused the light to shine out at "crazy angles". I then asked Charlie's mother if she had an extra disposable placemat, like the one she used at the restaurant. She did and she brought me one. It indeed was a very busy pattern and I could see why Charlie was unable to locate his food. To demonstrate, I placed it on his high chair tray and scattered his food, which just seconds before he was able to locate and now wasn't able to locate. I also explained to Charlie's mother that with the busy environment (people moving and unusual noises), it would make sense that Charlie was distracted from his meal. Finally, the unusual light hanging above the table was most likely a huge distraction for Charlie. His mother noted that he did stare at it throughout lunch and she had a difficult time redirecting him. Clearly, this story could have been placed in one of several CVI Strategy Areas (demonstrating difficulty in the area of Environmental and Sensory Input, Light, Contrast or difficulty with Visual Target). This example demonstrates that it is often not that the vision changes from day to day but the situation that the child is in from day to day changes.*

Primary books that have reflective qualities are often attractive to students who benefit from Level 2 Strategies. The child may not understand that a book tells a story, but there is great value in getting students looking at the book and helping with turning pages (see later Chapter on Literacy).

Students who benefit from Level 2 strategies (particularly those just entering Phase II) may still have difficulty with identification of pictures and understanding that pictures represent something. Students who visually function at about 6.5 or 7 on The CVI Range may start to make a transition from identifying their favored 3 dimensional toy or object to identifying a color photograph of that same favored toy or object. Presenting the color photo on a tablet works well because of the backlighting provided by the tablet.

Teacher/parent made books with matt finish color photographs of the students' favorite items work well for this stage of vision development (again, see the Chapter on Literacy).

When pictures are used in a book, they should be simple, one item in a photo with high contrast background, familiar and only one to a page.

Use color to highlight specific aspects and salient features of objects, shapes and print. Use of a red permanent pen or yellow highlighter works well.

Spatial Window of Visual Attention or Visual Array – Level 2

Students who benefit from Level 2 Strategies can often view 2, 3 or 4 well-spaced visual targets, especially if they are presented in the student's best field of view and against a high contrast background.

Contrast – Level 2

Students using Level 2 Strategies still require good color contrast when working with new to them targets or beginning new routines or lessons. With familiar or favored visual targets, they generally can tolerate less contrast. For example, if a student is very familiar with a lighted yellow ball, the yellow ball might be placed on a golden colored carpet and the student would most likely still visually locate it.

During bath time, use brightly colored Crayola bath soap or Crayola Bathtub Finger Paint Soap (in a tube or a tub) on solid colored (preferably white) tub walls and tile. Make sure to turn the child so that he/she is able to use the preferred visual field when playing with the paint soap on the tile walls.

Choose tablet applications that offer slow moving targets that stand out from their background. A good example of an application, which might be used with students who benefit from Level 2 Strategies, would be Tap-N-See Now or Big Bang Pictures.

Preferred Visual Field – Level 2

Since use of lower visual fields is often difficult for students with CVI, stairs are sometimes an obstacle. Use red, reflective strips to make stairs stand out.

As students become more mobile, use of red duct tape may help to outline doorways, mark the path in corridors as well as highlight steps (see Figure 7.1).

Use an Invisiboard (from APH which has a Velcro compatible surface), to affix targets to in the student's preferred visual field. Using a piece of dowel (spray painted black), you can affix Velcro on either end and extend it across a "U" shaped set up of the Invisiboard, so that targets can be hung from the dowel into the student's field of view.

An All-In-One Board (from APH which also has a Velcro compatible surface) can be set so it is in the right or left visual field as well as set centrally.

Students in wheelchairs can often be turned at an angle so that they might better use their preferred visual field while viewing Power Point presentations, Smart Board presentations or just viewing a white dry erase board.

Lighting – Level 2

Lighting continues to be an important factor to initiate looking behavior and to focus attention on the target of interest for the student who benefits from Level 2 Strategies.

Present visual targets on top of a Light Box from APH. Some Light Boxes can be slanted to bring targets better into the visual field. You can also download a light box app for a tablet or iPad. Brightly colored window gel stickers work well on both the Light Box and the light box app.

During bath time use a water safe, light up floating toy. These are often found at pool supply stores or online.

To encourage mobility, use a lighted orange safety cone (see Figure 6.1). Use the type that have both a blinking red light on the top and have a light inside. Move this cone to various locations around the room and turn on the light when it is time to move to the next location.

Use of a high-powered flashlight (with at least 300 lumens or greater) or supplementary desk light shining on visual targets will continue to be important.

Eliminate glare on all surfaces (do not laminate high-use targets!).

Dim overhead lights to emphasize lighted visual target; this also has the added benefit of seeming to reduce environmental clutter and complexity.

Familiarity – Level 2

Once teachers and others working with the student know of their favored visual targets, they can then take some quality of the favored visual target and "attach" it to a "new-to-the-student" visual target. For example, if one of the student's favored, familiar visual targets is a red, mylar pom pom, one could take a wide strip of red mylar ribbon and wrap it around a sip-n-seal cup to encourage the student to look for the cup, reach for it and then grasp it, just as he/she did with the pom pom.

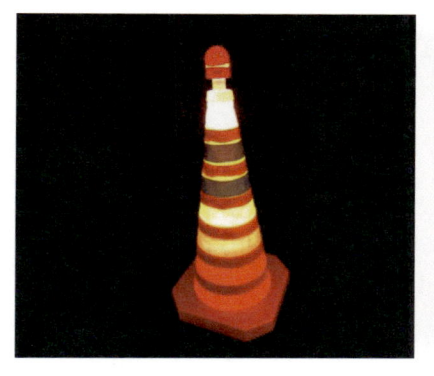

Figure 6.1 – Illuminated traffic safety cone, for distance viewing and mobility purposes

Figure 6.2 – Brightly colored eating utensils

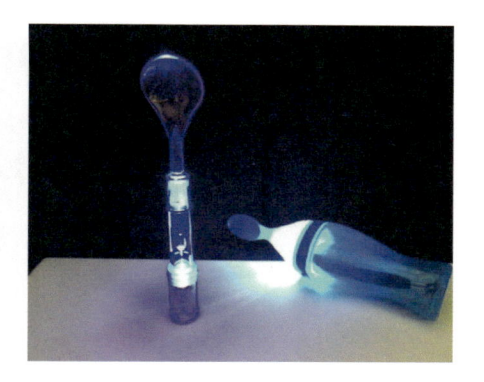

Figure 6.3 – Illuminated cutlery

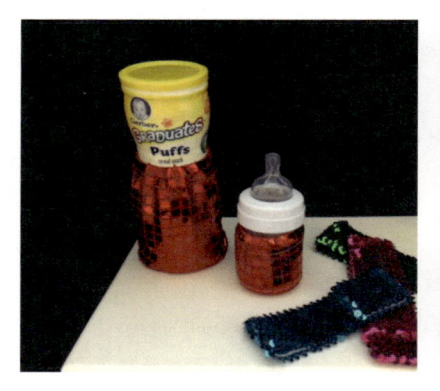

Figure 6.4 – Mylar-like fabric and sequined headbands for "Koozies"

Figure 6.5 – Brightly colored and illuminated plates and bowls

Figure 6.6 – Red light up double walled tumbler from www.flashingblinkinglights.com

Figure 6.7 – Red / Green recordable buttons

Chapter 7 - Level 3 CVI Strategies

General Considerations – Level 3

Students who benefit from Level 3 Strategies often demonstrate more typical visual behavior. However, they may continue to have difficulty with competing environmental and sensory input while trying to use their vision, especially when viewing targets at a distance. They may continue to have visual field preferences and often have difficulty viewing targets when at distance or presented in their lower visual field.

Students who benefit from Level 3 Strategies often continue to have difficulty with crowding, or the presentation of too many targets in their viewing array. This is particularly true when viewing distance targets because in some ways this is just another array with too many visual targets! Having a solid contrasting color in the viewing array is often helpful to the student trying to differentiate between background and foreground visual information. Lighting continues to be important, especially for mobility purposes.

Students using Level 3 Strategies will be responding to more varied visual targets and have greater visual demands. Be careful to watch for visual fatigue and allow plenty of response time for them to visually locate the target (especially if it is at distance), look at it and then respond to it.

Additional response time will especially be needed if the student is tired, stressed, ill, or has just had a seizure.

Be specific about what you want the student to look at.

Good communications between the school personnel and caretakers/parents at home will be crucial.

Use descriptive words and continue to discuss salient features of the visual target.

Continue to monitor pictures for "visual clutter" and use pictures that the student can clearly identify.

When a student benefits from Level 3 Strategies, it will be important for all teachers, paraprofessionals and caretakers to follow the same teaching procedures, both at school and at home. For example, if a yellow highlighter is used at school to mark where the student puts the answer on the answer line, this same technique should be used at home.

Environmental and Sensory Input – Level 3

A student who benefits from Level 3 strategies generally has more typical visual behaviors, but may continue to have difficulty with multiple sensory input, especially with competing auditory input. Parents, caretakers and teachers will need to watch carefully to determine how much competing sensory input the child is able to tolerate while still demonstrating efficient visual responses.

Visual complexity and crowding will most likely still be a concern especially if the student is in a Resource Room or classroom setting and using distance viewing to access information on a dry erase board or when mobile.

> *Molly, a 15-year-old high school student with a diagnosis of CP and brain damage related vision loss, seems to have little to no difficulty with most CVI behavioral characteristics. However, when needing to process information coming to her from multiple sensory channels, she is challenged and demonstrates difficulty. Between classes, when no other students are in the hallways, if asked to walk from her classroom to the gym, the clinic, down the stairs, or to the front office, Molly travels well in her familiar school setting locating the named destination with no difficulty or guidance. However, during the change of classes when the hallways are crowded with noisy students, moving quickly, causing bumps and pushes, Molly is less successful at using her vision efficiently. She resorts to using only auditory and tactual input, listening to guidance from her teachers as to where to go, and tactually trailing the wall with her hand. She takes only tiny steps, feeling her way with each step. Molly receives ongoing Orientation and Mobility Instruction for this area that she still has not resolved.*

Students may benefit from increased lighting on both near materials and in the general environment, such as in hallways and stairwells.

Students may still have difficulty with additional auditory and/or tactual distractions; limit these as able when visual learning is expected to take place.

When mobile in a busy, cluttered environment, it may be helpful to follow a line on the floor or hallway wall made with red duct tape (see Figure 7.1) or to look up to follow the line of lights on the ceiling.

When in PE, teammates may need to verbalize where the ball is ("Look by your foot").

Use of yellow or amber/orange-tinted sunglasses often help to make objects stand out, when outside in the bright sunlight.

Near/Middle/Distance Viewing – Level 3

A student who benefits from Level 3 Strategies may continue to have difficulty with distance viewing and strategies are often needed when visual learning is taking place at distance. Sometimes, the child with CVI functioning at this level will be in a regular classroom setting, Resource Room, or Life Skills Classroom, where there is often distance learning, particularly at the white board and/or Smart Board.

When students are in a classroom setting and are having difficulty seeing print targets on the dry erase board, use a yellow acetate sheet (similar to the one in the APH Light Box materials) outlined in red duct tape and placed over the print of interest (see Figure 7.2). It can be held to the dry erase board with a heavy-duty magnet. Alternately, use magnetic strips covered in red mylar wide ribbon to create a box around important information on the board (see Figure 7.3).

Distant targets (10-15 feet) will need to stand out in some way, especially when there is "visual clutter" surrounding the target of interest. Strategies to accomplish this could include use of;

> Color – An aid wearing a lighted red hat is easier to spot in a busy cafeteria (see Figure 7.4), a classmate can be found on a busy playground when he/she is in a bright, red shirt and a teacher holding a bright, yellow umbrella can be visually located when on a field trip
>
> Light – A high-powered flashlight shining on hands as they sign an assignment makes them easier to see for the student who has hearing difficulties in addition to CVI (see Figure 5.8)
>
> Movement – A waving flag at the top of a flagpole is easier to locate than a limp, still flag, drooping alongside a flagpole

Bright, florescent or bold colors will still draw student's attention.

Students may need to get up and get closer to materials and targets to reduce crowding and other visual distracters.

Continue to keep the work surface free of visual clutter (no notebooks, pens, cell phones, etc.).

When using a Power Point Presentation from the computer, use the movement of the cursor (displayed on the screen) to attract visual attention to a specific target – it causes a jumpy movement that is easy to spot at distance.

Continue to use color to draw attention to landmarks at greater distances. For example, if a student has a difficult time locating a doorway, use red rope lights running along the entire doorframe to mark the doorway or walkway, then, gradually, shorten the length (run rope light down just one side of the doorframe) then withdraw it altogether.

Use black "frames" to attract attention towards distance targets (use precut, black mat board frames from craft store; they come in various sizes). You can outline these in red mylar "garland" (see Figure 7.5).

When encouraging a student to look for a target in the distance, use a verbal prompt and a large visual target to "cue" the student to the chosen target ("Look at the big green tree then look for the teacher standing under it" or "Look at me, then look where my hand is pointing on the white board").

A student's table or desk will stand out at distance by attaching a yellow "ink blotter" on the workspace; keep the "blotter" in place with clear ConTac Paper.

A student's chair will stand out at distance by using a different color of chair from the other students or by attaching a brightly colored pom pom on the seat back.

Brightly colored distant PE equipment that has movement qualities will be easier to visually locate and see (i.e. swinging bright blue swing or a fluorescent colored ball or birdie).

Use the camera function on tablets to take pictures of distance targets (such as teacher notes) and then let the student use the zoom function to look at picture details.

Students in a classroom or Resource Room setting might benefit from use of a CCTV for distance viewing. The two I have found that work best for our students are the CCTVs that have a camera that can rotate and move to where the teacher is or to the specific board of interest. These include the SmartView 360 (www.humanware.com) and the Acrobat (www.enhancedvision.com).

Casey, a 7-year-old boy with a visual diagnosis of Cortical Visual Impairment, was learning how to swim during the summer months. I happened to run into Casey's mother and asked how the swimming lessons were coming along. She indicated that Casey was getting more comfortable in the water and learning how to push off the wall and float out to her. Casey's mom said that although Casey could float and was starting to take a few arm pulls, he didn't want her to move further away than about 6 feet because he couldn't see her. As we stood there in the store, we began to brainstorm and come up with a variety of ideas to solve this distance-viewing problem. We decided that she could wear a bright red, floppy sun hat while in the pool, to help Casey spot her and therefore hopefully she could move progressively further away, giving him more of a chance to use his arms and kick, to go along with his floating. A few weeks later when I saw Casey's mom I asked how the red hat strategy had worked. She enthusiastically reported that it worked very well and that Casey was now swimming! She said that in addition to wearing the red hat, she made some modifications to the pool deck and surrounding area. She had noticed, when she looked at the pool setting, that there were potted plants (red in color), lounge chairs and cushions, all creating complexity and visual clutter as well as other red targets in the background. So she decided to move everything from the background so that her red hat would be the only red to be seen, as Casey looked her direction. This was exactly the type of thinking I hope parents of my students learn and I was really pleased.

Visual Target – Level 3

Students who benefit from Level 3 Strategies may need books, worksheets, pictures and other two-dimensional materials modified.

Students may be starting to identify more pictures including color photographs, and simple, black line drawings.

Students in Life Skills classrooms or Resource Rooms may be using a Daily Calendar. Make a "CVI Friendly" Daily Calendar by taking photos of familiar items representing each daily activity (i.e. a picture of the student's familiar lunchbox to represent Lunch Time) and mounting them on small squares of black foam core board with Velcro on the back. Then, using an All-In-One Board, or other Velcro compatible slanted board, designate two columns; one with the heading, "Now", and one with the heading, "Next". Use only two of the photos at a time and use wide separation. When the "Now" activity is finished, the student can pull it down and put that one in the "Finished Basket" which may be a bright red or bright yellow bin. The student can then move the "Next" photo over to the "Now" column and set another picture into place for "Next" (see figure 7.6).

Eliminate details that are not important to the page (e.g. use correction fluid on all page numbers, use correction fluid on all but the outer black outline of pictures, etc).

When looking at multiple shapes, numbers or letters, encourage the student to track with their finger; point to each symbol and slide the finger from target to target.

Use color
- Outline letters or numbers with a red permanent marker
- Highlight aspects and salient features of shapes, objects, and print with a colorful highlighter
- Highlight the answer line on worksheets (be consistent in the use of one color on all answer lines/worksheets)
- Place over picture or word a yellow overlay or yellow transparency (it makes the letters "pop" out in sharp contrast)
- Pastel colored pictures could be outlined with a permanent marker and re-colored with bright primary colors

- Use individual colored tote boxes for specific items; blank paper in one colored tote and completed assignments in another colored tote, etc.
- Clearly mark the beginning and end of a line of print with marker or highlighter (use green marker outlining first letter in line – red marker outlining last letter in line; or use colored stick-on dots – a green dot to mark the beginning of the line and a red dot to mark the end of the line)
- Use colorful/reflective contact paper to stick on and outline targets of interest
- Use a highlighter or re-usable highlighter tape to run vertically down the left side of the paper, to encourage students with left field difficulties to begin scanning (or printing or reading) at the far left side of the paper

Simplify visual targets to help reduce the "crowding phenomenon";
- Use window markers to emphasize a visual target of interest (cut a "window" in black construction paper to outline the target of interest)
- Use Bright Line Markers (from APH) and/or wide black paper markers
- Use correctional fluid to eliminate details that are distracting and unnecessary
- Cut or fold worksheets and papers to allow only small parts to show at a time, reducing the amount of information presented

Students might benefit from modifications in PE equipment including the use of brightly colored balls, beanbags, and birdies. Use brightly colored bases for baseball and encourage teammates to all wear the same brightly colored tee shirts, making them easier to locate on the field.

Students in a classroom or Resource Room setting often benefit from use of a CCTV for near viewing. As noted above, the two I have found that work best for our students include the SmartView 360 (www.humanware.com) and the Acrobat (www.enhancedvision.com). These CCTVs allow the student to enlarge the near target and to adjust the background color to suit their needs.

Spatial Window of Visual Attention or Visual Array – Level 3

The spacing of visual targets in the visual array may continue to be important. Teachers, caretakers and parents may still need to reduce crowding and complexity as students are able to view greater numbers of targets.

Special attention will need to be paid to any augmentative and alternative communication (AAC) aid and/or device that the student might be using. Many commercially made aids and devices have spaces for 9 to 20 small pictures. Even for a student who can use Level 3 Strategies, this array is often still too busy and cluttered. In addition, the pictures most often used with these devices are inappropriate (see information on pictures under Targets). A more appropriate AAC device might be a teacher made aid or a voice output device that only has 2 or 3 windows. Alternately, black paper can be placed in windows and only a few window choices can be offered, which will create a less busy array (see the "TalkBar" from Learning Resources).

If the student is a beginning reader, it will be important to use a program with large spaces between words and pictures. The Primary Phonics (K-2) series is a good example (see Chapter on Literacy).

Use books with one clear, simple picture on a contrasting simple background.

Develop custom worksheets and provide good spacing between words and between sentences. This is often simply achieved by creating modified worksheets on a computer.

Limit the number of words and/or sentences on a page.

Create more white space by using correction fluid, folding the paper to hide "visual clutter" and enlarging the pater on a photocopy machine. Also use blocking techniques by taking a black piece of heavy tag board and blocking off non-necessary visual details.

Encourage the student to keep items on the desk to a minimum; emphasize organization.

Encourage the student to keep books and materials organized in bright, color-coded folders inside of the desk. Folders now come in mylar-like material or sparkle materials.

Contrast – Level 3

Students who benefit from Level 3 Strategies generally can tolerate more complexity surrounding the target of interest at near, but often continue to have difficulty with targets at distance. They still need the distance targets to stand out in some way with either color, movement, light or with an auditory cue.

George, a student who was in a Life Skills program at the high school level, generally did quite well using his vision to locate targets at distance, even when there was little or no contrast. While visiting his classroom, his teacher asked me if I could walk over to the gym to watch George in PE. They had started a new unit and he was having difficulty participating. I walked over and found the group playing badminton, and George was indeed having difficulty locating the birdie. When I stood next to George and watched as the birdie approached him, I realized that the white birdie did not stand out in any way due to the white ceiling and the white walls in the gymnasium. Furthermore, the glare from the overhead lights caused the white birdie to virtually disappear! I returned the next day with fluorescent orange birdies. His coach adjusted the overhead lights and where George stood (in relation to the lights), and classmates started giving verbal cues to George, as the birdie approached him. These simple modifications helped him immensely and he was able to participate with his teammates in this fun game.

Students using Level 3 strategies who use a CCTV will benefit from the models that allow a choice of background contrasting color.

Students often benefit from PowerPoint presentations when the target on the screen is a bright color and the template used is a darker color.

When creating student specific books on a tablet, use applications that offer a variety of background colors and text colors. A good example of an application to use is *Book Creator*.

Preferred Visual Field – Level 3

Present targets in student's preferred visual field:
- Allow student to move materials where they can see them most efficiently
- Allow student to move their body to where they can see the materials most efficiently
- Determine if student views materials more efficiently in horizontal plane or vertical plane
- Use a slant board or reading stand
- Create your own custom made slant board to fit specific wheelchair trays
- Allow student to tilt or turn his/her head to the best angle for viewing targets and for reading.

Students using a tablet can bring the tablet up into their preferred field of view by using a stand similar to the Tablet Combo Stand in Figure 7.7 (www.rjcooper.com).

When mobile (either walking or in a wheelchair), the student may need to turn his/her head all the way downward, due to lower visual field difficulties.

Position the student so he/she is better able to use their preferred visual field. For example, if they are better able to use their far right visual field, they should be sitting towards the left side of the classroom.

When mobile and using stairs, watch for lower visual field difficulties; mark stairs with red duct tape or red reflective tape.

When mobile, travel in brightly lit hallways and stairwells. Use supplementary lights to illuminate dark stair wells.

Work on use of a "slow, look, check, and go" method combined with verbal prompts, or a tap on the shoulder, when there is uneven ground and/or there is a concern with lower visual field.

Lighting – Level 3

Working in a well-lit environment will continue to be beneficial.

For students in Resource Room settings or regular classroom settings, it is helpful to attach a small battery powered light inside of the book section of the desk or locker, to help the student locate needed books and supplies.

Watch for shadows as student bends over work; seat the student under overhead lights so that shadows are not cast on their near work.

Use of a small, battery-powered desk light is helpful for students moving from class to class, especially when they need additional supplementary lighting on their near materials, and access to a wall plug is unavailable,

Use a PowerPoint Presentation to teach concepts; dim overhead lights, use programs that have movement qualities and in Slide Show view, turn your mouse into a laser pointer to draw your student's visual attention. You can also change the color of your laser pointer on the Slide Show tab.

Eliminate glare on computer monitors and workspace.

Use of an LED Illuminated Dry Erase Board is helpful for beginning readers. The fluorescent-like markings stand out well (see Figure 7.8).

When using an electric desk light, remember to seat students near a wall outlet, when possible.

Familiarity – Level 3

Usually, by the time the student is working with Level 3 Strategies, they have little to no difficulty with Familiarity.

Figure 7.1 – Red duct tape marking for mobility

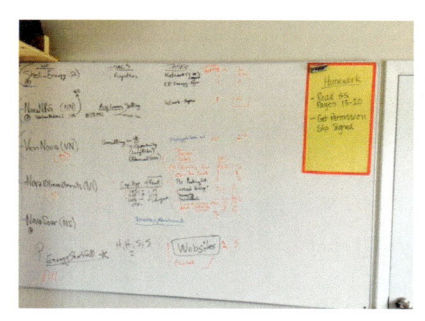

Figure 7.2 – Yellow acetate trimmed in red duct tape

Figure 7.3 – Red mylar magnetic strips

Figure 7.4 – Red light-up hat www.flashyblinkylight.com

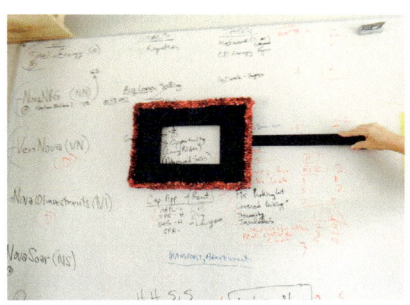

Figure 7.5 – Black mat frame with red mylar "garland"

Figure 7.6 – Daily Schedule or Daily Calendar

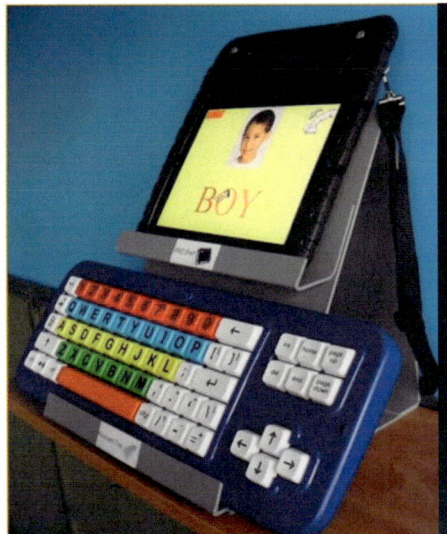

Figure 7.7 – Tablet combo stand www.rjcooper.com

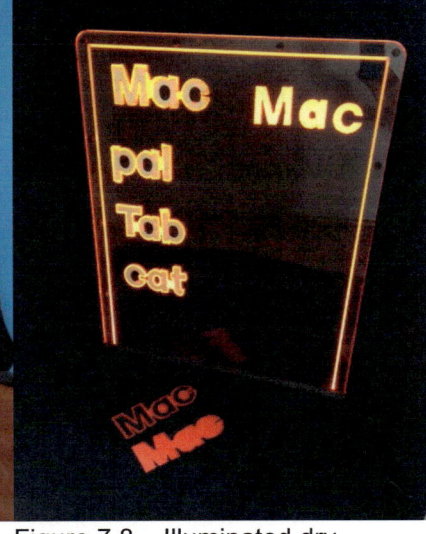

Figure 7.8 – Illuminated dry erase board

Chapter 8 - Additional Areas to Consider

Visual Fatigue

Watch for visual fatigue. Signs of visual fatigue include, but are not limited to, yawning, fading attention, irritability, crying and sleepiness.

Take note of the conditions in which visual fatigue occurs.

Note how long the student can use their vision efficiently before visual fatigue occurs.

Research any ocular condition the student may have in addition to CVI. Certain ocular conditions cause visual fatigue, including astigmatism.

Note which modifications and/or accommodations help to reduce visual fatigue.

Encourage frequent breaks.

Positioning

Ensure that the student is in a comfortable, secure position when efficient use of vision is the goal.

Do not try a new stander or chair (or other new position) when working on use of vision. The student is working hard to use the new device and may not have the energy to devote to using vision efficiently.

Work closely with the PT or therapist to determine the best position to help the student feel secure and comfortable. Determine if there is a specific chair or table/tray that works best for the student.

Note which position allows the student to use his or her arms and/or hands most efficiently.

Note if overhead lights or window lights need to be considered when positioning the student. Glare can often be easily eliminated by proper positioning.

Reduce or eliminate unintentional body movement when visual learning is expected to take place. This is especially true for a student who is just beginning to use their vision. A child who is in a wheelchair, but not properly belted in or in an inappropriately fitted chair, may slide down, slide to the side, or her head may fall to one side. A child who is feeling like they are falling out of their chair is not going to be visually attending to a target or using their vision efficiently!

When a child's head rolls to one side, the visual field involuntarily shifts; provide appropriate head support

Try a variety of positions to determine which one may best support visual attending behaviors

Eye/Hand Use

There will be some students, especially those who benefit from Level 1 Strategies, who may have difficulty with or lack use of their hands/arms.

Note whether the student uses a look/reach/grasp behavior when looking at targets or if he uses a look/look away/reach and grasp behavior when looking at a target (i.e. if look and touch occur simultaneously or not).

Some students are able to use eye gaze to communicate. Many of the discussed strategies may then apply.

Chapter 9 - CVI Skills Inventory & Strategies Worksheet

The following CVI Skills Inventory & Strategies Worksheet is meant to help decide which strategies could be helpful for encouraging students with CVI to more consistently and efficiently use their vision.

Background Information

Before completing the CVI Skills Inventory & Strategies Worksheet, it is advisable for the student to have a Functional Vision Evaluation (FVE) and Learning Media Assessment (LMA) completed. This would include information on the student's visual functioning level on The CVI Range and whether the student is functioning in Phase I, Phase II or Phase III. As noted at the beginning of this book, Strategies in Level 1, Level 2 and Level 3 loosely correlate with the visual functioning levels of students in Phase I, Phase II and Phase III of The CVI Range.

The front page of the CVI Skills Inventory & Strategies Worksheet should be completed as thoroughly as possible. Special attention should be paid to whether the student is on any medications, note any possible side effects of those medications, and whether there is any hearing loss. In addition, note whether the student experiences seizures and whether the student has a shunt (blinking lights and close proximity to a tablet are sometimes contraindicated for students in these two categories).

Completion of the CVI Skills Inventory & Strategies Worksheet

First, read through the three levels of skills for each of the 8 CVI Strategy Areas. If the student has the skill, circle "Yes"; if the student does not have the skill, circle "No". These three skills, within each CVI Strategy Area, correlate <u>loosely</u> with the three levels of strategies; the first box with Level 1 Strategies, the second with Level 2 Strategies and the third with Level 3 Strategies. This will guide you when choosing strategies.

Next, observe the child throughout the day and determine activities of the Core Curriculum or Expanded Core Curriculum that are impacted as a result of difficulty with this Strategy Area. Note these activities or learning situations to the right of the "Yes" and "No" column for each CVI Strategy Area.

Moving to the next box to the right, decide upon interventions, strategies and recommendations, which might encourage more efficient use of vision, given each impacted activity. As noted above, the circled "Yes" or "No" will **guide you** in selecting and developing strategies. For example, if your student has "Yes" circled next to the first skill in a CVI Strategy Area, but "No" circled for the next two, you might look at examples of ideas in Level 2 CVI Strategies. The following are guidelines for determining the Level of Strategies to use;

- If the first "No" is circled within a CVI Strategy Area (followed by "No" in the second and third box), look at Level 1 Strategies
- If the first "Yes" is circled within a CVI Strategy Area (followed by "No" for the second and third box), look at Level 2 CVI Strategies
- If the first "Yes" and the second "Yes" are circled within a CVI Strategy Area (followed by "No" for the third box"), look at Level 3 CVI Strategies.
- If all three of the "Yes" boxes are circled, there may be very little use of strategies needed or possibly, none. For example, in the CVI Strategy Area of Familiarity, a student who visually functions in Phase III may have all three boxes circled, "Yes", and therefore may not need any modifications in this area.

In the last column on the far right, check which, if any, Expanded Core Curriculum areas are addressed given the activities that are impacted and the interventions that are suggested. This will help you when completing IEP and ARD forms at annual meetings.

Once all 8 CVI Strategy Areas have been addressed, look at the Additional Areas To Consider. Make notes in these areas, as appropriate.

Once this CVI Skills Inventory & Strategies Worksheet is fully completed, it will help with development of the PLAAFP and IEP Goals and Objectives, which will be discussed in the next chapter.

CVI Skills Inventory & Strategies Worksheet

Student Name _____ Sex ____ Age/DOB _____ Date _____

TVI Name _____ **Program** (check all that apply)

Address _____ ____ Homebound ____ PPCD ____ Self Cont.
School District
_____ ____ Lifeskills ____ ECI ____ Other
Street
_____ ____ Gen. Ed. ____ Resource Room
City   State   Zip

CVI Range: _____ Circle One: Phase I   Phase II   Phase III

Background Medical History and Information (check all that apply)

_____ Premature Birth	_____ Low Birth Weight	_____ PVL
_____ Anoxia	_____ Hypoxic-Ischemic Encephalopathy (HIE)	_____ IVH (grade ___)
_____ Developmental Delay	_____ Cerebral Palsy	_____ ROP
_____ Intracranial Hemorrhage/Stroke	_____ Brain Malformations	_____ TBI
_____ CNS Infections	_____ Hydrocephalic/Shunt	_____ Other
_____ Seizures/Epilepsy	_____ CVI	_____ Other

Ophthalmologist _____ Address _____ Current Eye Report/Date _____
Diagnosis _____

Optometrist _____ Address _____ Current Eye Report/Date _____
Diagnosis _____

Low Vision Specialist _____ Address _____ Current Eye Report/Date _____
Diagnosis _____

Hearing/Medications

Documentation on Hearing _____ ABR _____

Current Otological Examination (date) _____ Current Audiological Examination (date) _____

Medications (list all prescription medications & possible visual side effects for each) _____
_____
_____

Current Special Education Eligibilities and/or Support Services (check all that apply)

____ OHI   ____ VI   ____ AI   ____ D/B   ____ OI   ____ SI   ____ ID
____ O&M   ____ ABM ____ OT   ____ PT   ____ Other (list) _____, _____, _____

© VeriNova, 2011-2016. All rights reserved.   StrategyToSee.com

CVI Strategy Areas		Has Skill (yes or no)	Activity(ies) that Strategy Area Impacts Observe student in one or more of the following areas to determine impact: Independent Living, Orientation and Mobility, Recreation/Leisure, Self-Determination, Sensory Efficiency, Social Interaction, Compensatory/Access, AT/Technology, Career Education, Fine/Gross Motor, PE, Speech and Language, and all areas of the Core Curriculum.
Environmental/Sensory Input	Able to attend to visual target(s) when all environmental and sensory input is controlled.	yes	
		no	
	Attends to visual target(s) during quiet background noise/voices and/or minor tactual input	yes	
		no	
	No difficulty visually attending to target(s) in typical multi-sensory environment (as in a typical preschool setting)	yes	
		no	
Near/Middle/Distance Viewing	Attends to visual target(s) up to 36 inches	yes	
		no	
	Attends to visual target(s) up to 6-10 feet away	yes	
		no	
	Attends to visual target(s) up to 10-20 feet away	yes	
		no	
Visual Target	Visually attends to single/solid colored or lighted target(s) only	yes	
		no	
	Visually attends to target(s) of 2-3 colors, simple pictures, or simple color photographs	yes	
		no	
	Visually attends to educational materials (worksheets/books) with typical print and pictures for age	yes	
		no	

© VeriNova, 2011-2016. All rights reserved.

StrategyToSee.com

Interventions, Strategies, and Recommendations Which Might Encourage More Efficient Use of Vision in this CVI Strategy Area	ECC Areas Addressed
	___AT/Tech ___Career Ed. ___Comp./Access ___Ind. Liv. Skills ___O & M ___Rec./Leisure ___Self-Det. ___Sensory Eff. ___Soc. Inter.
	___AT/Tech ___Career Ed. ___Comp./Access ___Ind. Liv. Skills ___O & M ___Rec./Leisure ___Self-Det. ___Sensory Eff. ___Soc. Inter.
	___AT/Tech ___Career Ed. ___Comp./Access ___Ind. Liv. Skills ___O & M ___Rec./Leisure ___Self-Det. ___Sensory Eff. ___Soc. Inter.

© VeriNova, 2011-2016. All rights reserved.

StrategyToSee.com

CVI Strategy Areas		Has Skill (yes or no)	Activity(ies) that Strategy Area Impacts Observe student in one or more of the following areas to determine impact: Independent Living, Orientation and Mobility, Recreation/Leisure, Self-Determination, Sensory Efficiency, Social Interaction, Compensatory/Access, AT/Technology, Career Education, Fine/Gross Motor, PE, Speech and Language, and all areas of the Core Curriculum.
Spatial Window of Visual Attention and/or Viewing Array	Visually attends to one or two widely spaced visual target(s) at near (with good color contrast)	yes	
		no	
	Visually attends to 3-10 well spaced visual targets at near and/or distance (note distance and if SpotLighting, highlighting, or high contrast is needed)	yes	
		no	
	No difficulty attending to multiple targets at near and/or distance (no difficulty with "visual clutter" and/or poor contrast)	yes	
		no	
Contrast	Attends to near visual target(s) when presented against a solid colored background	yes	
		no	
	Attends to near visual target(s) when presented against multiple colors/ patterns	yes	
		no	
	Attends to visual target(s) in foreground and at distance with typical home/ classroom "visual clutter" in background	yes	
		no	

© VeriNova, 2011-2016. All rights reserved.

StrategyToSee.com

Interventions, Strategies, and Recommendations Which Might Encourage More Efficient Use of Vision in this CVI Strategy Area	ECC Areas Addressed
	___AT/Tech ___Career Ed. ___Comp./Access ___Ind. Liv. Skills ___O & M ___Rec./Leisure ___Self-Det. ___Sensory Eff. ___Soc. Inter.
	___AT/Tech ___Career Ed. ___Comp./Access ___Ind. Liv. Skills ___O & M ___Rec./Leisure ___Self-Det. ___Sensory Eff. ___Soc. Inter.

CVI Strategy Areas		Has Skill (yes or no)	Activity(ies) that Strategy Area Impacts Observe student in one or more of the following areas to determine impact: Independent Living, Orientation and Mobility, Recreation/Leisure, Self-Determination, Sensory Efficiency, Social Interaction, Compensatory/Access, AT/Technology, Career Education, Fine/Gross Motor, PE, Speech and Language, and all areas of the Core Curriculum.
Preferred Visual Field	Attends to visual target(s) at far left and/or far right visual field, approximately eye height at near	yes	
		no	
	Attends to visual target(s) in far left, far right, and/or central visual fields (limited or no attending lower visual field)	yes	
		no	
	Attends to visual target(s) in all visual fields including lower visual field	yes	
		no	
Lighting	Visually attracted to light; stares or stared at light source (i.e. sunlight or electric light)	yes	
		no	
	Visually attracted to light (or reflective targets) but can be redirected to other visual targets	yes	
		no	
	Visually attends to lights and non-lighted visual targets equally well. No staring at light sources noted	yes	
		no	
Familiarity	Attends to very familiar visual target(s) or target(s) student has looked at over and over	yes	
		no	
	Will look at target(s) that have been adapted with a quality that is favored or familiar (i.e. reflective mylar attached)	yes	
		no	
	No target preference; attends to all targets, familiar and unfamiliar, equally well	yes	
		no	

© VeriNova, 2011-2016. All rights reserved.　　　　StrategyToSee.com

Interventions, Strategies, and Recommendations Which Might Encourage More Efficient Use of Vision in this CVI Strategy Area	ECC Areas Addressed
	___AT/Tech ___Career Ed. ___Comp./Access ___Ind. Liv. Skills ___O & M ___Rec./Leisure ___Self-Det. ___Sensory Eff. ___Soc. Inter.
	___AT/Tech ___Career Ed. ___Comp./Access ___Ind. Liv. Skills ___O & M ___Rec./Leisure ___Self-Det. ___Sensory Eff. ___Soc. Inter.
	___AT/Tech ___Career Ed. ___Comp./Access ___Ind. Liv. Skills ___O & M ___Rec./Leisure ___Self-Det. ___Sensory Eff. ___Soc. Inter.

Additional Areas to Consider

Visual Fatigue

1. Does this student experience visual fatigue? Signs of visual fatigue may include, but not be limited to, yawning, fading attention, irritability, sleepiness, and crying.

2. Describe conditions in which visual fatigue occurs.

3. How long is this student able to use their vision efficiently before visual fatigue occurs?

4. Certain ocular conditions cause visual fatigue including astigmatism. Does this student have an ocular condition (in addition to CVI), which may cause visual fatigue?

5. What modifications or accommodations help to reduce visual fatigue?

Positioning

1. What is the best position for this student to be in while using vision? Consider meeting with the physical therapist, who can often give valuable advice on the best position for your student.

2. Which position allows this student to use his/her arms most efficiently? For example, it might be leaning forward over a round bolster cushion.

3. Is there a specific chair and/or table/tray that works best with this student?

4. Do overhead lights or window light need to be considered when positioning this student? Will the position of the student cause a shadow on materials to be viewed?

Eye/Hand Use

1. Is this student able to use his/her arms/hands to reach for objects?

2. Does this student look at a target, then while looking at it, reach for or grasp the target (i.e. look and touch occur simultaneously)?

3. Does this student look at a target, then look away and reach for or grasp the target (i.e. look and touch do not occur simultaneously)?

4. What modifications will encourage look and touch to occur simultaneously? Consider reducing multi-sensory input, limiting number of targets, creating high contrast between target and background, SpotLighting target, and placement of target.

Notes

Sample of Completed CVI Skills Inventory & Strategies Worksheet for a Student who Benefits from Level 1 Strategies

The following is a CVI Skills Inventory & Strategies Worksheet that was completed for a student who benefits from Level 1 Strategies and who has functional vision at approx. 1-2 on The CVI Range. Amy was just beginning to use her vision when this Worksheet was completed. Amy was born prematurely and has a significant neurological history. She was diagnosed as hydrocephalic and had an Intraventricular Hemorrhage, grade IV both sides (IVH). She has seizures and currently has a shunt. Note the precautions on the back of the form with regard to use of an iPad and students with shunts. Amy also has a documented "mild hearing loss", however, during the evaluation period she seemed to use her hearing quite well. Her mother planned to take her for a follow up appointment with the Audiologist.

CVI Skills Inventory & Strategies Worksheet

Student Name Amy   **Sex** F   **Age/DOB** 16 mo.   **Date** _____

TVI Name Ms. Seewell

Program (check all that apply)

Address Friendly ISD (School District)

- ✓ Homebound
- ___ PPCD
- ___ Self Cont.
- ___ Lifeskills
- ✓ ECI
- ___ Other
- ___ Gen. Ed.
- ___ Resource Room

CVI Range: 1-2   **Circle One:** (Phase I)   Phase II   Phase III

Background Medical History and Information (check all that apply)

✓ Premature Birth	___ Low Birth Weight	___ PVL
___ Anoxia	___ Hypoxic-Ischemic Encephalopathy (HIE)	✓ IVH (grade 4)
✓ Developmental Delay	___ Cerebral Palsy	___ ROP
___ Intracranial Hemorrhage/Stroke	___ Brain Malformations	___ TBI
___ CNS Infections	✓ Hydrocephalic/Shunt	___ Other
✓ Seizures/(Epilepsy)	___ CVI	___ Other

Ophthalmologist Dr. Eyesight   **Address** _____   **Current Eye Report/Date** June 2014

Diagnosis Cortical Visual Impairment, left exotropia and optic nerve atrophy

Optometrist _____   **Address** _____   **Current Eye Report/Date** _____

Diagnosis _____

Low Vision Specialist _____   **Address** _____   **Current Eye Report/Date** _____

Diagnosis _____

Hearing/Medications

Documentation on Hearing: Mild hearing loss, bilaterally   **ABR** no

Current Otological Examination (date) _____   Current Audiological Examination (date) _____

Medications (list all prescription medications & possible visual side effects for each) _____

No prescription medications taken on a regular basis

Current Special Education Eligibilities and/or Support Services (check all that apply)

- ___ OHI
- ✓ VI
- ___ AI
- ___ D/B
- ___ OI
- ✓ SI
- ✓ ID
- ___ O&M
- ___ ABM
- ✓ OT
- ✓ PT
- ___ Other (list) ___, ___, ___

CVI Strategy Areas		Has Skill (yes or no)	Activity(ies) that Strategy Area Impacts Observe student in one or more of the following areas to determine impact: Independent Living, Orientation and Mobility, Recreation/Leisure, Self-Determination, Sensory Efficiency, Social Interaction, Compensatory/Access, AT/Technology, Career Education, Fine/Gross Motor, PE, Speech and Language, and all areas of the Core Curriculum.
Environmental/Sensory Input	Able to attend to visual target(s) when all environmental and sensory input is controlled.	yes / no (yes)	-When parents present a stuffed toy for Amy to play with, she is distracted by and attends only to the barking dog. -When Amy's mom plays with her, she uses a soothing voice as she places an object in Amy's hand. When Amy drops it, she doesn't search or even briefly search, but attends only to her mother's voice. -During feeding time, the television is on and Amy clearly listens to it. As the spoon full of food approaches, she does not visually notice the spoon is approaching, but only alerts as her mother touches the edge of the spoon on her lips. Then Amy opens her mouth to accept the food.
	Attends to visual target(s) during quiet background noise/voices and/or minor tactual input	yes / no (no)	
	No difficulty visually attending to target(s) in typical multi-sensory environment (as in a typical preschool setting)	yes / no (no)	
Near/Middle/Distance Viewing	Attends to visual target(s) up to 36 inches	yes / no (no)	-During playtime, Amy's mother moved a toy slowly in front of Amy at a distance of approx. 36 inches and Amy did not visually respond or track the moving target. -When Amy's mother walked in front of her, Amy did not alert to the movement or track her movement. -During playtime, as Amy was on her tummy on a patterned baby quilt, she was encouraged to scoot towards a multicolored toy near several other toys, but she did not seem interested.
	Attends to visual target(s) up to 6-10 feet away	yes / no (no)	
	Attends to visual target(s) up to 10-20 feet away	yes / no (no)	
Visual Target	Visually attends to single/solid colored or lighted target(s) only	yes / no (yes)	-Amy does not look at her mother or father's faces. She attends well to their voices but never looks at their faces. -When an object is placed in Amy's hand, she does not visually inspect or examine the object.
	Visually attends to target(s) of 2-3 colors, simple pictures, or simple color photographs	yes / no (no)	
	Visually attends to educational materials (worksheets/books) with typical print and pictures for age	yes / no (no)	

© VeriNova, 2011-2016. All rights reserved. StrategyToSee.com

Interventions, Strategies, and Recommendations Which Might Encourage More Efficient Use of Vision in this CVI Strategy Area	ECC Areas Addressed
-During playtime, if Amy is expected to use her vision, get the dog to be quiet, turn off the TV, turn off music and limit talking. Present single colored toys and targets, one at a time, against a solid contrasting color in her preferred visual field. SpotLIGHT the target, if needed. -Although Amy's doctor has noted a mild hearing loss, she seems to attend to auditory input quite efficiently, so when you want her to use her vision, be as quiet as possible. When Amy drops a toy or it rolls out of reach, give her a touch cue if needed. If she begins to look toward the objects, a verbal cue can be used like a reward to encourage more looking behavior. -During feeding time, turn the TV off. Amy alerts well to lighted objects, therefore, use a light up spoon and bring it into her field of view on the right side, which is her preferred visual field. A good spoon to use would be a Munchkin Easy Squeezy Spoon modified with a small flashlight inside of it.	___AT/Tech ___Career Ed. ✔Comp./Access ___Ind. Liv. Skills ___O & M ___Rec./Leisure ___Self-Det. ✔Sensory Eff. ___Soc. Inter.
-Amy seems to respond best to visual targets when they are within arm's reach or less than 28 inches away. She actually responds most frequently when targets are about 12 to 18 inches away. Remember to use single colored, brightly colored targets and targets and objects that light up. -Amy is drawn to lighted targets and bright, single colors (no patterns). Therefore, wear a large, bright red tee shirt and possibly a red-lighted necklace. Walk in front of Amy starting at her far right side and keep the distance no greater than 3 feet away. -Use a quilt or baby blanket that is a solid color, preferably black. Use a brightly colored toy, such as red or yellow (single color only, no patterns), that when placed on the blanket, really stands out. Present only that one toy on the blanket and use SpotLIGHTing techniques if needed. When the multicolored toy was presented on the patterned quilt, the toy seemed to blend into the pattern and was difficult for Amy to visually locate.	___AT/Tech ___Career Ed. ✔Comp./Access ___Ind. Liv. Skills ___O & M ✔Rec./Leisure ___Self-Det. ✔Sensory Eff. ✔Soc. Inter.
-To get Amy to attend to your face, try using red, lighted glasses (www.flashingblinkylights.com) at specific times every day (like diaper changing time). Turn down the overhead lights when you have these glasses on and do not talk or have other sounds competing for her attention. Note; do not use the blinking feature on the glasses as this might set off a seizure. Another idea would be to wear bright red lipstick and slowly move your mouth in Amy's near right field of view. Or, wear a mylar-like red fabric scarf around the hair. Creating some kind of high contrast "Edge", with regard to the face will encourage looking behavior. -To encourage Amy to be more visually inquisitive, place objects that light up in her hand. An easy object to hold is a plastic Energizer emergency light stick (get at the hardware stores). They come in a variety of colors, but red might be best. Press the button to get a steady light, instead of the blinking light (sometimes blinking lights set off seizures)	___AT/Tech ___Career Ed. ✔Comp./Access ___Ind. Liv. Skills ___O & M ___Rec./Leisure ___Self-Det. ✔Sensory Eff. ✔Soc. Inter.

CVI Strategy Areas		Has Skill (yes or no)	Activity(ies) that Strategy Area Impacts Observe student in one or more of the following areas to determine impact: Independent Living, Orientation and Mobility, Recreation/Leisure, Self-Determination, Sensory Efficiency, Social Interaction, Compensatory/Access, AT/Technology, Career Education, Fine/Gross Motor, PE, Speech and Language, and all areas of the Core Curriculum.
Spatial Window of Visual Attention and/or Viewing Array	Visually attends to one or two widely spaced visual target(s) at near (with good color contrast)	(yes)	
		no	
	Visually attends to 3-10 well spaced visual targets at near and/or distance (note distance and if SpotLighting, highlighting, or high contrast is needed)	yes	-During playtime, Amy is placed on her back under a baby gym/activity gym. Amy doesn't seem to notice the hanging toys in the gym and does not interact with the toys. -During bath time, many floating toys are around Amy, but she doesn't interact with them. -When two brightly colored objects are presented to Amy, she does not shift her visual attention between the two.
		(no)	
	No difficulty attending to multiple targets at near and/or distance (no difficulty with "visual clutter" and/or poor contrast)	yes	
		(no)	
Contrast	Attends to near visual target(s) when presented against a solid colored background	(yes)	
		no	
	Attends to near visual target(s) when presented against multiple colors/ patterns	yes	-During mealtime, many Cheerios are placed on Amy's tray, but she has difficulty locating them visually. -When a toy or object is presented to Amy by mom (who was wearing a multicolored blouse), Amy does not notice the toy. -During playtime, Amy does not play with her hands or her feet, or seem to notice they are there.
		(no)	
	Attends to visual target(s) in foreground and at distance with typical home/ classroom "visual clutter" in background	yes	
		(no)	

© VeriNova, 2011-2016. All rights reserved. StrategyToSee.com

Interventions, Strategies, and Recommendations Which Might Encourage More Efficient Use of Vision in this CVI Strategy Area	ECC Areas Addressed
−Instead of using a baby gym, use a "CVI Den" with only one hanging, lighted toy that is within reach for Amy. Use a black 'Repel Sleep Screen' to create a "CVI Den". A Repel Sleep Screen is a lightweight travel mosquito repellant screen used mostly by campers, but can be modified to create contrast and hang toys from, for a student with CVI. The black, mesh dome can be placed over the student, but caregivers can still see through to monitor the student's use of vision. (Or, see "Bug Hut 1 Pro Shelter" at www.rei.com) −During bath time, wait until the water has filled the tub before placing Amy in the tub. Keep auditory input to a minimum and use a toy in a bright, solid color (yellow floating duck). Use only one toy or object at a time. Alternately, use a light up orb or LED ball (often used for floating in a pool). −When presenting objects to Amy, make certain there is good color contrast behind the targets. Wear a black smock or use an Invisiboard. Use objects that light up in a solid color, like red, yellow or purple. Use a brief auditory cue or tactual cue, if necessary, to draw visual attention to one of the objects.	___AT/Tech ___Career Ed. ✓Comp./Access ___Ind. Liv. Skills ___O & M ___Rec./Leisure ✓Self-Det. ✓Sensory Eff. ___Soc. Inter.
−Amy's high chair tray is light tan in color and when Cheerios are placed on the tray, they appear to be the same color and blend in. Always present objects and targets against a high contrast background. In addition, Amy has more difficulty viewing targets in her lower visual field (see preferred visual field below). −Creating high contrast between the object of interest and the background will be especially important at this stage of encouraging Amy to use her vision. Whoever is playing with Amy may need to put on a black smock or wear a solid colored shirt (i.e. keep handy an extra large, black tee shirt to slip on when working with Amy). When a toy is presented to Amy in front of a multicolored shirt, it "disappears" against its background. −Amy will need to be encouraged to explore her hands and feet by drawing her visual attention to them. Use a brightly colored bracelet or light up bracelet will encourage looking behavior towards the hand or ankle. Highlight one hand or ankle at a time. Use of a FlashBanz in red (from www.flashingblinkylights.com) or sequined or mylar-like 'slap bracelet'. Other reflective material cuffs could be SpotLIGHTed.	___AT/Tech ___Career Ed. ✓Comp./Access ✓Ind. Liv. Skills ___O & M ___Rec./Leisure ✓Self-Det. ✓Sensory Eff. ___Soc. Inter.

CVI Strategy Areas		Has Skill (yes or no)	Activity(ies) that Strategy Area Impacts Observe student in one or more of the following areas to determine impact: Independent Living, Orientation and Mobility, Recreation/Leisure, Self-Determination, Sensory Efficiency, Social Interaction, Compensatory/Access, AT/Technology, Career Education, Fine/Gross Motor, PE, Speech and Language, and all areas of the Core Curriculum.
Preferred Visual Field	Attends to visual target(s) at far left and/or far right visual field, approximately eye height at near	(yes) / no	-When a brightly lit toy was moved into Amy's field of view on her left side, she did not respond to it. -When Amy's mother sat on Amy's left side to feed her, Amy did not notice the spoon full of food as it was coming into her field of view. -When Cheerios were presented on the tray of Amy's high chair, she had difficulty locating them.
	Attends to visual target(s) in far left, far right, and/or central visual fields (limited or no attending lower visual field)	yes / (no)	
	Attends to visual target(s) in all visual fields including lower visual field	yes / (no)	
Lighting	Visually attracted to light; stares or stared at light source (i.e. sunlight or electric light)	(yes) / no	-When encouraging Amy to bang a toy on her high chair tray, Amy repeatedly looked at/stared at the window where bright sunlight was pouring through. -During play time, when Amy was on her back on the baby blanket, rather than attending to the toys her mother was presenting to her, she stared at the overhead ceiling light.
	Visually attracted to light (or reflective targets) but can be redirected to other visual targets	yes / (no)	
	Visually attends to lights and non-lighted visual targets equally well. No staring at light sources noted	yes / (no)	
Familiarity	Attends to very familiar visual target(s) or target(s) student has looked at over and over	(yes) / no	-When Amy's ophthalmologist was examining Amy, he used a multi-patterned toy to try to gain her visual attention (per mom). She did not notice the target. -Amy's grandmother gave Amy a soft, stuffed toy that had a butterfly pattern on it, but Amy wouldn't look at it.
	Will look at target(s) that have been adapted with a quality that is favored or familiar (i.e. reflective mylar attached)	yes / (no)	
	No target preference; attends to all targets, familiar and unfamiliar, equally well	yes / (no)	

Interventions, Strategies, and Recommendations Which Might Encourage More Efficient Use of Vision in this CVI Strategy Area	ECC Areas Addressed
-Present all objects and materials on Amy's far right side, at eye height and within 28 inches. -During feeding time, parents and caregivers should sit on Amy's right side and present food starting in Amy's far right visual field at eye height at near. Move the spoon or food in a slow steady movement, moving inward towards Amy's central visual field. Use a light up spoon and turn Amy away from bright, sunny windows. May need to turn the room light lower. -Difficulties with lower visual field are common. Raising targets up into the preferred visual field often helps to alleviate this problem. Use an All-In-One Board and place it at a 45-degree angle. Cheerios will "grip" the Velcro compatible side and will stand out against the black fabric. Present only two well spaced Cheerios at a time. Use SpotLIGHTing techniques to draw attention to the target.	✓ AT/Tech ___ Career Ed. ✓ Comp./Access ✓ Ind. Liv. Skills ___ O & M ___ Rec./Leisure ✓ Self-Det. ✓ Sensory Eff. ___ Soc. Inter.
-When visual learning is expected to take place, turn Amy away from the window where sunlight is coming through. Avoid having Amy face windows with Levolor blinds, or stripes of light, coming into the room. -Turn the overhead ceiling light off and keep the room slightly darkened, when working on visual tasks with lighted toys and objects.	___ AT/Tech ___ Career Ed. ___ Comp./Access ___ Ind. Liv. Skills ___ O & M ___ Rec./Leisure ___ Self-Det. ✓ Sensory Eff. ___ Soc. Inter.
-When attending any ophthalmologist, optometrist or low vision specialist appointment, remember to take familiar, consistently looked at targets that Amy consistently responds to. This may included lighted toys and targets. -Make sure to let grandparents and other family members know of appropriate visual targets that Amy will be more likely to look at and interact with. Send out a Wish List for Amy just before holidays and birthday, which will give them a better idea of appropriate toys.	___ AT/Tech ___ Career Ed. ___ Comp./Access ___ Ind. Liv. Skills ___ O & M ✓ Rec./Leisure ___ Self-Det. ✓ Sensory Eff. ✓ Soc. Inter.

Additional Areas to Consider

Visual Fatigue

1. Does this student experience visual fatigue? Signs of visual fatigue may include, but not be limited to, yawning, fading attention, irritability, sleepiness, and crying.
Yes. Amy demonstrates a fading of attention when visually fatigued.

2. Describe conditions in which visual fatigue occurs.
Amy will lose interest in visual targets or fade when expected to use her vision for a length of time

3. How long is this student able to use their vision efficiently before visual fatigue occurs?
Amy can use her vision for short, 5-10 minute periods throughout the day.

4. Certain ocular conditions cause visual fatigue including astigmatism. Does this student have an ocular condition (in addition to CVI), which may cause visual fatigue?
No, this student does not have an ocular condition that might cause visual fatigue.

5. What modifications or accommodations help to reduce visual fatigue?
Encourage use of vision for many short periods of time throughout the day, during naturally occurring routines.

Positioning

1. What is the best position for this student to be in while using vision? Consider meeting with the physical therapist, who can often give valuable advice on the best position for your student.
Amy seems to feel most secure and comfortable when she is seated in her high chair, with two rolled hand towels used as props wedged in on either side of her.

2. Which position allows this student to use his/her arms most efficiently? For example, it might be leaning forward over a round bolster cushion.
When Amy's arms are on her high chair tray, she is most able to use her arms and hands.

3. Is there a specific chair and/or table/tray that works best with this student?
Nothing specific at this time, except her high chair with rolled towels.

4. Do overhead lights or window light need to be considered when positioning this student? Will the position of the student cause a shadow on materials to be viewed?
Amy is still very drawn towards bright sunlight and overhead lights. She should be positioned so that her back is towards the window. Overhead lights should be turned down or turn Amy away from overhead lights.

Eye/Hand Use

1. Is this student able to use his/her arms/hands to reach for objects?
Yes, Amy is just starting to use her hands to reach for and grasp objects.

2. Does this student look at a target, then while looking at it, reach for or grasp the target (i.e. look and touch occur simultaneously)?
No, look and touch do not occur simultaneously.

3. Does this student look at a target, then look away and reach for or grasp the target (i.e. look and touch do not occur simultaneously)?
Yes, Amy looks towards the target, and then looks away as she reaches towards the target.

4. What modifications will encourage look and touch to occur simultaneously? Consider reducing multi-sensory input, limiting number of targets, creating high contrast between target and background, SpotLighting target, and placement of target.
SpotLIGHTing a target when it is presented against a contrasting color will encourage Amy to look and touch simultaneously.

Notes

Since Amy has a history of seizures, avoid using blinking or flashing lights. However, since Amy is attracted to light, use a steady light source to encourage looking and grasping behavior. Use SpotLIGHTing techniques.

Amy has a programmable valve setting in her shunt. Since external magnetic programming tools can change programmable valve settings by interacting with a magnetic rotor inside the valve, use of the iPad at close range (less than 3 inches away) is not advised. Several studies have suggested that exposure to tablet devices, such as an iPad 2, may alter programmable shunt valve settings.

Sample of Completed CVI Skills Inventory & Strategies Worksheet for a Student who Benefits from Level 2 Strategies

The following is a CVI Skills Inventory & Strategies Worksheet that was completed for a student who benefits from Level 2 Strategies and who has functional vision at approx. 5-6 on The CVI Range. Will has a visual diagnosis of Cortical Visual Impairment, secondary to complications from Anoxia at birth. Will also has a diagnosis of Cerebral Palsy. He is in a Life Skills classroom setting and there are approximately 12 other students in his classroom. There is a teacher and two paraprofessionals who all alternate working with Will. Will is in a wheelchair and he has very limited to no use of his right hand and limited functional use of his left arm and hand.

CVI Skills Inventory & Strategies Worksheet

Student Name Will   **Sex** M **Age/DOB** 9 yrs **Date** Fall 2014

TVI Name Ms. Seewell   **Program** (check all that apply)

Address Friendly ISD   ___ Homebound ___ PPCD ___ Self Cont.
School District
                                                      ✓ Lifeskills ___ ECI ___ Other
Street
                                                      ___ Gen. Ed. ___ Resource Room
City   State   Zip

CVI Range: 5-6   Circle One: Phase I   (Phase II)   Phase III

Background Medical History and Information (check all that apply)

___ Premature Birth	___ Low Birth Weight	___ PVL
✓ Anoxia	___ Hypoxic-Ischemic Encephalopathy (HIE)	___ IVH (grade ___)
___ Developmental Delay	✓ Cerebral Palsy	___ ROP
___ Intracranial Hemorrhage/Stroke	___ Brain Malformations	___ TBI
___ CNS Infections	___ Hydrocephalic/Shunt	___ Other
___ Seizures/Epilepsy	✓ CVI	___ Other

Ophthalmologist Dr. Eyesight   **Address** _____   **Current Eye Report/Date** _____

Diagnosis: Cortical Visual Impairment, nystagmus, optic atrophy. Dr. Eyesight has recommended a Low Vision Evaluation

Optometrist _____   **Address** _____   **Current Eye Report/Date** _____

Diagnosis _____

Low Vision Specialist _____   **Address** _____   **Current Eye Report/Date** _____

Diagnosis _____

Hearing/Medications

Documentation on Hearing: Hearing screened by school nurse 09/03/2014. Results were within normal limits; both ears   **ABR** _____

Current Otological Examination (date) _____   Current Audilogical Examination (date) _____

Medications (list all prescription medications & possible visual side effects for each) _____
No prescription medications taken on a regular basis

Current Special Education Eligibilities and/or Support Services (check all that apply)

___ OHI   ___ VI   ___ AI   ___ D/B   ___ OI   ✓ SI   ✓ ID
___ O&M   ___ ABM   ✓ OT   ✓ PT   ✓ Other (list) Adaptive PE , _____

CVI Strategy Areas		Has Skill (yes or no)	Activity(ies) that Strategy Area Impacts Observe student in one or more of the following areas to determine impact: Independent Living, Orientation and Mobility, Recreation/Leisure, Self-Determination, Sensory Efficiency, Social Interaction, Compensatory/Access, AT/Technology, Career Education, Fine/Gross Motor, PE, Speech and Language, and all areas of the Core Curriculum.
Environmental/Sensory Input	Able to attend to visual target(s) when all environmental and sensory input is controlled.	(yes) no	–During breakfast, several students eat breakfast while Will works on the computer, just on the other side of the breakfast table. After breakfast, the paraprofessional runs the vacuum cleaner. When it was turned on, Will startled and was very distracted. He was unable to get back to his task for several minutes after the vacuum cleaner was turned off. –During Direct Instruction (Identification of Numbers/Letters/Colors), movement of students walking by on either side of Will made it difficult for him to stay on task. Once he looked up to see who was walking by, it took some time to get him looking back and visually locating the materials. –During Daily Calendar Time, when a PowerPoint Presentation was on the screen, the other students' movement caused Will's wheelchair to be bumped. Each time the wheelchair was bumped, Will looked to see who bumped his chair.
	Attends to visual target(s) during quiet background noise/voices and/or minor tactual input	yes (no)	
	No difficulty visually attending to target(s) in typical multi-sensory environment (as in a typical preschool setting)	yes (no)	
Near/Middle/Distance Viewing	Attends to visual target(s) up to 36 inches	(yes) no	–During Independent Activities/Motor Skills, Will is in his modified rolling chair (Tumble Forms/Feeder Seat) and has difficulty tracking the movement of the small, multicolored ball as it comes towards him from a distance of about 6 – 8 feet. There are generally many other children playing with balls all around him during this period. –During Daily Calendar, Will has difficulty visually locating and attending to the pointer stick (the big, white finger) pointing to the large calendar, which is about 6 feet away. –During Daily Calendar/Days of the Week, Will has difficulty visually locating and attending to the Months of the Year section of the board, which is also about 6 feet away.
	Attends to visual target(s) up to 6-10 feet away	yes (no)	
	Attends to visual target(s) up to 10-20 feet away	yes (no)	
Visual Target	Visually attends to single/solid colored or lighted target(s) only	(yes) no	–When working on his Daily Calendar, there are many Board Maker pictures representing all daily activities. Will has difficulty discerning their meaning and knowing which picture to move to the "finished" section of the notebook. –When working on ELA, flash cards are presented to Will flat on the table. He is to choose the requested letter by touching it. The flashcards are made up from white squares of paper with letters marked by hand in pencil. Will often doesn't look at the letters and without looking, touches the letter closest to his left hand, as he is better able to use his left hand.
	Visually attends to target(s) of 2-3 colors, simple pictures, or simple color photographs	(yes) no	
	Visually attends to educational materials (worksheets/books) with typical print and pictures for age	yes (no)	

© VeriNova, 2011-2016. All rights reserved.　　　　StrategyToSee.com

Interventions, Strategies, and Recommendations Which Might Encourage More Efficient Use of Vision in this CVI Strategy Area	ECC Areas Addressed
-Move laptop computer to a different location in the room, away from the breakfast eating area. Only start the vacuum cleaner during the change of activity, when there is more noise and movement naturally. -Direct Instruction should be in an area of the classroom where no other students will walk by. Utilizing the corner area that is somewhat empty might be a good option. Turn Will's back to the classroom and have him and his desk facing the corner. Take down the existing bulletin board materials to create a plain, blank wall. -During Daily Calendar, encourage other students to leave space between where they are sitting and Will's wheelchair.	___AT/Tech ___Career Ed. ✓Comp./Access ___Ind. Liv. Skills ___O & M ___Rec./Leisure ___Self-Det. ✓Sensory Eff. ___Soc. Inter.
-Use a large red and yellow Rib-It Ball from APH (18 or 30 inch models). Make sure that other balls are cleared out so that the Rib-It Ball is the only one in the field of view and it stands out. Make sure that Will is facing the blank wall at the end of the gym, which is low in visual clutter. Put your face down near his face, to see what the field of view looks like, to insure that all visual clutter is cleared. Make sure that Will visually locates the ball before it is rolled towards him by providing some movement (shake the ball) or an directional auditory cue ("look down by my feet"). Finally, roll the ball slowly towards him. -Use a pointer stick/pointer finger that lights up (Learning Resources) or use a piece of red, mylar-like "garland" on the end of the pointer so that it is easier for Will to see. Alternately, provide Will with his own personal calendar and personal pointer finger. The calendar could be an APH Individual Calendar, which is modified with black lines and color, or an APH Class Calendar, which is modified. Insure high contrast between numbers and background. Use plain, block numbers such as found in APH's font called APHont. APHont was developed specifically for students with low vision. -Get Will as close to the board as possible when working on the months of the year. Remove all "visual clutter" surrounding the months-of-the-year section of the board (or use black form board to cover up "visual clutter"). Use a black "window frame" to outline the specific month you expect Will to be looking at. Use slight movement of the "window frame" or an auditory cue to bring his visual attention to the month of interest.	___AT/Tech ___Career Ed. ✓Comp./Access ✓Ind. Liv. Skills ___O & M ✓Rec./Leisure ___Self-Det. ✓Sensory Eff. ___Soc. Inter.
-Instead of using BoardMaker pictures, use real color photographs of familiar objects and targets, such as Will's lunchbox, which can represent the daily activity, "Lunch". Attach the color photographs to a square of black foam core, which has Velcro on the back. Use an Invisiboard or All-In-One Board and create two sections; A "NOW" section and a "NEXT" section. Using only two familiar pictures at a time to represent activities happening "Now" and activities happening "Next" will be much easier for Will and the sturdy foam core will be helpful when he pulls them off of the board to put into a separate, bright yellow, "Finished" basket. -Create flashcards from black, heavy cardstock and use a die-cut machine to create block letters from bright, yellow cardstock. Glue the yellow letters onto the black flashcards. Present only 2 choices of letters at a time. Present the letters on a slant board or attach two well-spaced flashcards to an All-In-One Board. Use clothespins that have been spray-painted black and have Velcro compatible backing to hold materials on to the All-In-One Board.	___AT/Tech ___Career Ed. ✓Comp./Access ✓Ind. Liv. Skills ___O & M ___Rec./Leisure ___Self-Det. ✓Sensory Eff. ___Soc. Inter.

CVI Strategy Areas		Has Skill (yes or no)	Activity(ies) that Strategy Area Impacts Observe student in one or more of the following areas to determine impact: Independent Living, Orientation and Mobility, Recreation/Leisure, Self-Determination, Sensory Efficiency, Social Interaction, Compensatory/Access, AT/Technology, Career Education, Fine/Gross Motor, PE, Speech and Language, and all areas of the Core Curriculum.
Spatial Window of Visual Attention and/or Viewing Array	Visually attends to one or two widely spaced visual target(s) at near (with good color contrast)	**yes** no	
	Visually attends to 3-10 well spaced visual targets at near and/or distance (note distance and if SpotLighting, highlighting, or high contrast is needed)	yes **no**	-At near, Will generally does well visually with 2-5 well-spaced targets at near, but has more difficulty with 6-10 or more targets at near and multiple distance targets (36 inches or further away). When discussing the weather during Daily Calendar, Will has difficulty locating and attending to the Weather Chart and it's individual symbols (sunny, rain, snow, etc.). With multiple targets on the chart, the array is busy, and it is usually about 4 to 6 feet away. -During Social Studies, many community signs are shown on the Smart Board, such as a stop sign, a yield sign, a green traffic light, etc. Will has difficulty locating the requested sign when many are shown on the board together. In addition, when Will uses the plastic pointer "finger" to touch the screen, the touch interactive surface doesn't respond.
	No difficulty attending to multiple targets at near and/or distance (no difficulty with "visual clutter" and/or poor contrast)	yes **no**	
Contrast	Attends to near visual target(s) when presented against a solid colored background	**yes** no	-During snack time, Will is given several bite sized pieces of Fiber One Fruit Flavored Snack, pieces of banana, and pieces of a Mozzarella cheese stick. These snack pieces are presented on a tan paper towel. Often, Will tactually locates his bits of food, rather than using vision, then reaching and grasping. Sliding of the paper towel makes the process more challenging. -During Computer Time, Will often uses a program called Switch Skills 1. In one of the cause and effect programs, Will has to watch the movement of a soccer ball on the laptop screen (which is 24 to 36 inches away) and press a Mac switch when the soccer ball comes onto the monitor (which could be in a variety of locations). Will sometimes has difficulty locating the soccer ball and misses his opportunity to hit the Mac Switch. -During Adaptive PE, Will sometimes has difficulty locating a purple foam ball when the teacher tosses it to him from a distance of 3 or 4 feet. The ball, on the day of observation, was the exact same color as the instructors shirt.
	Attends to near visual target(s) when presented against multiple colors/patterns	yes **no**	
	Attends to visual target(s) in foreground and at distance with typical home/classroom "visual clutter" in background	yes **no**	

© VeriNova, 2011-2016. All rights reserved.

StrategyToSee.com

Interventions, Strategies, and Recommendations Which Might Encourage More Efficient Use of Vision in this CVI Strategy Area	ECC Areas Addressed
-With regard to the Weather Chart, create a "Window Frame" with multiple frames, to divide up the chart. Each type of weather can be shown within it's own "Frame". Use black foam core material to cut out the frames. Move Will to within 24 inches of the board. Angle his wheelchair so that he can better use his right visual field. Allow him to answer "yes" when the pointer finger touches the correct weather for the day. -When using the Smart Board, present only 2 to 3 community signs at a time. Make sure that there is good spacing between each sign and that signs used are bright in color and stand out from the background. Turn the overhead lights low so that the Smart Board images stand out. Turing the lights low also helps to reduce complexity and visual clutter surrounding the Smart Board. Attach a universally compatible capacitive Smart Board stylus onto the end of the class pointer, and work with Will's OT to attach this to his Velcro "glove". Using this technique, Will should be able to use the interactive Smart Board screen along with his classmates.	___AT/Tech ___Career Ed. ✔Comp./Access ✔Ind. Liv. Skills ___O & M ___Rec./Leisure ✔Self-Det. ✔Sensory Eff. ___Soc. Inter.
-Encourage more efficient use of vision by presenting bits of food on a non-slip, contrasting surface. You can use a large, scooper plate with suction-type base or a non-slip "placemat" cut from Dycem. Make sure that any plate or placemat used is of a bold color that will create contrast for the food on it. When appropriate, present foods on a slightly slanted board, such as the All-In-One Board. Foods that cling well on a slightly slanted All-In-One Board include foods with a gritty/rough texture like Cheerios. -When using cause and effect programs on the computer, have an Invisiboard behind the computer monitor, to eliminate multiple colors, patterns and "visual clutter". This helps to make the monitor stand out and makes it easier for Will to locate the moving soccer ball. -To help create contrast between the purple ball used in adaptive PE and the purple shirt worn by the instructor, the instructor could put on a long, black smock. The purple ball will then stand out as he encourages Will to visually locate it and track it's movement as it is tossed to him.	✔AT/Tech ___Career Ed. ✔Comp./Access ✔Ind. Liv. Skills ___O & M ___Rec./Leisure ___Self-Det. ✔Sensory Eff. ___Soc. Inter.

CVI Strategy Areas		Has Skill (yes or no)	Activity(ies) that Strategy Area Impacts Observe student in one or more of the following areas to determine impact: Independent Living, Orientation and Mobility, Recreation/Leisure, Self-Determination, Sensory Efficiency, Social Interaction, Compensatory/Access, AT/Technology, Career Education, Fine/Gross Motor, PE, Speech and Language, and all areas of the Core Curriculum.
Preferred Visual Field	Attends to visual target(s) at far left and/or far right visual field, approximately eye height at near	(yes) / no	-At near, Will attends well to targets presented in his right, left and central visual fields. When viewing distant targets (4 to 6 feet away, he seems to have more difficulty viewing targets on his left side, particularly when seated on the left side of the circle during Daily Calendar. -During ELA when working on shapes, students passing by bumped into the table causing the All-In-One Board to slide and move out of Will's field of view. In addition, the flashcards were propped up on the All-In-One Board. Therefore when the table was bumped, the flashcards slid down, again out of Will's preferred field of view.
	Attends to visual target(s) in far left, far right, and/or central visual fields (limited or no attending lower visual field)	(yes) / no	
	Attends to visual target(s) in all visual fields including lower visual field	yes / (no)	
Lighting	Visually attracted to light; stares or stared at light source (i.e. sunlight or electric light)	(yes) / no	-During Daily Calendar, when Jack Hartman's Counting To 100 (from You Tube) was on, Will seemed to have difficulty seeing the numbers on the screen in this Power Point Presentation. The glare on the screen (caused by the overhead lights) and the large amount of "visual clutter" all around the screen may both have contributed to Will's lack of visual attention to the program. -During Computer Time, sometimes the laptop monitor is tilted at an angle that creates glare. This makes it difficult for Will to visually attend to. -As noted previously, Will has a difficult time during Independent Activities/Motor Skills visually locating and tracking the movement of a rolling ball.
	Visually attracted to light (or reflective targets) but can be redirected to other visual targets	(yes) / no	
	Visually attends to lights and non-lighted visual targets equally well. No staring at light sources noted	yes / (no)	
Familiarity	Attends to very familiar visual target(s) or target(s) student has looked at over and over	(yes) / no	
	Will look at target(s) that have been adapted with a quality that is favored or familiar (i.e. reflective mylar attached)	(yes) / no	-Will generally looks at most targets. Certain pictures, including Board Maker pictures and pictures of stick figures, are often difficult for him to identify.
	No target preference; attends to all targets, familiar and unfamiliar, equally well	yes / (no)	

© VeriNova, 2011-2016. All rights reserved.   StrategyToSee.com

Interventions, Strategies, and Recommendations Which Might Encourage More Efficient Use of Vision in this CVI Strategy Area	ECC Areas Addressed
-Position Will so that he is sitting on the far right side of the circle during Daily Calendar, so that it is easier for him to use his right viewing field. -Use a non-skid material (such as Dycem) under the All-In-One Board to help it stay put. Use clothespins that have been spray-painted black and have Velcro compatible backing to hold materials securely on to the All-In-One Board. Alternately, use the APH Shapeboard Kit with only 1 to 3 shapes at a time. Mount the Shapeboard on an All-In-One Board so that it isn't laying flat on the table.	___AT/Tech ___Career Ed. ✓Comp./Access ___Ind. Liv. Skills ___O & M ___Rec./Leisure ___Self-Det. ✓Sensory Eff. ✓Soc. Inter.
-When showing a PowerPoint Presentation, turn the overhead lights off. This reduces glare and helps to "hide" visual clutter surrounding the screen. It also makes the individual lighted numbers in the PowerPoint Presentation "Pop" out. -Always look at targets from the student's perspective, especially to catch glare on surfaces that you might not see from where you are standing. Reduce glare on laptop screens by tilting them to create the most contrast and least amount of glare. -Use SpotLIGHTing techniques (in a dimly lit environment, when possible) to shine a bright spotlight on a rolling ball. This makes the ball stand out and easier for the student to visually locate and track. Use a high-powered flashlight, 250 lumens or greater, to spotlight targets. Avoid shining the light in student's eyes.	✓AT/Tech ___Career Ed. ✓Comp./Access ___Ind. Liv. Skills ___O & M ✓Rec./Leisure ___Self-Det. ✓Sensory Eff. ✓Soc. Inter.
-Use color photographs with a matt finish whenever possible. The photographs should be of single, familiar items presented against a solid colored background. Presenting photographs on the iPad, in programs such as Pictello, often works well for students with CVI.	✓AT/Tech ___Career Ed. ✓Comp./Access ___Ind. Liv. Skills ___O & M ___Rec./Leisure ___Self-Det. ✓Sensory Eff. ___Soc. Inter.

Additional Areas to Consider

Visual Fatigue

1. Does this student experience visual fatigue? Signs of visual fatigue may include, but not be limited to, yawning, fading attention, irritability, sleepiness, and crying.

Yes. Signs that Will is experiencing visual fatigue include, "looking off into space", inattentiveness, losing visual focus, and giving inaccurate answers to questions.

2. Describe conditions in which visual fatigue occurs.

Visual fatigue for Will usually happens after he has worked hard all morning and then after lunch he seems to fade.

3. How long is this student able to use their vision efficiently before visual fatigue occurs?

Will can usually use his vision for about 5 hours before he tires, but watch for signs of visual fatigue.

4. Certain ocular conditions cause visual fatigue including astigmatism. Does this student have an ocular condition (in addition to CVI), which may cause visual fatigue?

No, this student does not have an ocular condition that might cause visual fatigue.

5. What modifications or accommodations help to reduce visual fatigue?

Overall suggestions would include reducing visual clutter in all arrays, using lighted visual targets when able (as with PowerPoint Presentations) and reduce and/or eliminate distance viewing. Try to complete most of the Core Curriculum and Expanded Core Curriculum activities during the morning hours. After lunch, provide frequent breaks when visual tasks are being completed and use materials in auditory format, when appropriate.

Positioning

1. What is the best position for this student to be in while using vision? Consider meeting with the physical therapist, who can often give valuable advice on the best position for your student.

The best position for Will to be in when using his vision is sitting in his adapted NXT wheelchair.

2. Which position allows this student to use his/her arms most efficiently? For example, it might be leaning forward over a round bolster cushion.

Will only uses his left arm and hand. He is best able to use it while sitting upright in his wheelchair.

3. Is there a specific chair and/or table/tray that works best with this student?

Visual targets are often presented on the tray on Will's wheelchair. However, this tray is transparent. Since you can see through the tray, when targets are on the tray, you can also see Will's legs, pants, shoes, and down to the pattern on the floor. This often creates more "visual clutter" in the viewing field. It is often helpful to use a specially cut "placemat" that is of a contrasting color (black) and fits exactly on the tray.

4. Do overhead lights or window light need to be considered when positioning this student? Will the position of the student cause a shadow on materials to be viewed?

The overhead lights often cause glare for Will. Teachers and caretakers will need to watch for glare (from Will's point of view) and if needed, reposition materials or reposition Will. Eliminate glare whenever possible.

Eye/Hand Use

1. Is this student able to use his/her arms/hands to reach for objects?

Yes, Will can use his left hand in a raking motion to grasp items.

2. Does this student look at a target, then while looking at it, reach for or grasp the target (i.e. look and touch occur simultaneously)?

Look and touch only occasionally occur simultaneously.

3. Does this student look at a target, then look away and reach for or grasp the target (i.e. look and touch do not occur simultaneously)?

Yes, this student does initially look at the target, then as he looks away he reaches for it.

4. What modifications will encourage look and touch to occur simultaneously? Consider reducing multi-sensory input, limiting number of targets, creating high contrast between target and background, SpotLighting target, and placement of target.

Since Will only uses his left hand, placement of objects and food in his central or left field of view is often helpful.

Notes

Sample of Completed CVI Skills Inventory & Strategies Worksheet for a Student who Benefits from Level 3 Strategies

The following is a CVI Skills Inventory & Strategies Worksheet that was completed for a student who benefits from Level 3 Strategies and who has functional vision at approx. 7-8 on The CVI Range. Gina has a visual diagnosis of Cortical Visual Impairment, secondary to complications from Anoxia shortly after birth. She attends classes both in a Resource Room setting (for ELA and Math) and in the general education setting. She is working on resolution of CVI Behavioral Characteristics

CVI Skills Inventory & Strategies Worksheet

Student Name Gina   **Sex** F   **Age/DOB** 12 yr   **Date** _____

TVI Name Ms. Seewell

Address Friendly ISD   *School District*

_____ *Street*

_____ *City / State / Zip*

Program (check all that apply)
- ___ Homebound   ___ PPCD   ___ Self Cont.
- ___ Lifeskills   ___ ECI   ___ Other
- ✓ Gen. Ed.   ✓ Resource Room

CVI Range: 7-8   Circle One: Phase I   Phase II   **(Phase III)**

Background Medical History and Information (check all that apply)

- ___ Premature Birth
- ✓ Anoxia
- ___ Developmental Delay
- ✓ Intracranial Hemorrhage/**(Stroke)**
- ___ CNS Infections
- ✓ **(Seizures)**/Epilepsy
- ___ Low Birth Weight
- ___ Hypoxic-Ischemic Encephalopathy (HIE)
- ___ Cerebral Palsy
- ___ Brain Malformations
- ___ Hydrocephalic/Shunt
- ✓ CVI
- ___ PVL
- ___ IVH (grade ___)
- ___ ROP
- ___ TBI
- ___ Other
- ___ Other

Ophthalmologist Dr. Eyesight   **Address** _____   **Current Eye Report/Date** June 2014
Diagnosis Cortical Visual Impairment, optic atrophy

Optometrist _____   **Address** _____   **Current Eye Report/Date** _____
Diagnosis _____

Low Vision Specialist _____   **Address** _____   **Current Eye Report/Date** _____
Diagnosis _____

Hearing/Medications

Documentation on Hearing: Within normal limits per school nurse   ABR _____

Current Otological Examination (date) _____   Current Audiological Examination (date) _____

Medications (list all prescription medications & possible visual side effects for each) _____
Student takes no prescription medicaations on a regular basis. Past history of seizures has been resolved

Current Special Education Eligibilities and/or Support Services (check all that apply)

- ✓ OHI
- ✓ VI
- ___ AI
- ___ D/B
- ___ OI
- ✓ SI
- ___ ID
- ✓ O&M
- ___ ABM
- ___ OT
- ___ PT
- ___ Other (list) ___, ___, ___

© VeriNova, 2011-2016. All rights reserved.   StrategyToSee.com

CVI Strategy Areas		Has Skill (yes or no)	Activity(ies) that Strategy Area Impacts Observe student in one or more of the following areas to determine impact: Independent Living, Orientation and Mobility, Recreation/Leisure, Self-Determination, Sensory Efficiency, Social Interaction, Compensatory/Access, AT/Technology, Career Education, Fine/Gross Motor, PE, Speech and Language, and all areas of the Core Curriculum.
Environmental/Sensory Input	Able to attend to visual target(s) when all environmental and sensory input is controlled.	(yes) / no	-During ELA in the Resource Room, when students pass by and bump into Gina's chair/desk, she startles and becomes completely distracted from the task at hand. It often takes several minutes for her to get back on track and visually attend. -During independent work time, when Gina's Resource Room teacher is instructing a student who is near to Gina's desk, Gina often has difficulty visually attending to her task as she listens to instruction and interaction of others. -During lunchtime in the cafeteria, Gina often has difficulty locating her assigned table. This seems to be partly due to the great amount of auditory input (she is distracted), and also to distance viewing difficulties. All of the tables look the same to Gina and she has no idea where her specific table is.
	Attends to visual target(s) during quiet background noise/ voices and/or minor tactual input	(yes) / no	
	No difficulty visually attending to target(s) in typical multi-sensory environment (as in a typical preschool setting)	yes / (no)	
Near/Middle/Distance Viewing	Attends to visual target(s) up to 36 inches	(yes) / no	-During PE when the students are playing badminton, Gina often has difficulty tracking the movement of and seeing the birdie as it approaches. -During science, when the regular education teacher writes notes on the dry erase board, Gina has a difficult time locating the notes and then copying from the board, even though she is seated no more than 10 feet from the board. -In the Resource Room, Gina has difficulty seeing the sample math problems on the dry erase board.
	Attends to visual target(s) up to 6-10 feet away	yes / (no)	
	Attends to visual target(s) up to 10-20 feet away	yes / (no)	
Visual Target	Visually attends to single/solid colored or lighted target(s) only	(yes) / no	-In social studies class, when maps with keys and legends are used, Gina often has difficulty with small maps, many colors and varied keys. -In science class, when Gina is expected to gain information from pictures, she often has difficulty discerning what the picture represents.
	Visually attends to target(s) of 2-3 colors, simple pictures, or simple color photographs	(yes) / no	
	Visually attends to educational materials (worksheets/books) with typical print and pictures for age	yes / (no)	

© VeriNova, 2011-2016. All rights reserved.

StrategyToSee.com

Interventions, Strategies, and Recommendations Which Might Encourage More Efficient Use of Vision in this CVI Strategy Area	ECC Areas Addressed
-The Resource Room teacher can develop an alternate walking pathway in a different area from Gina's workspace. Set up a room divider/curtain to block student movement, especially on Gina's right side. -Ask the Resource Room teacher to conduct one-on-one instruction with other students away from Gina's workspace. Turn Gina's desk so that she has her back to this one-on-one interaction. -Ask the custodian to set out a red, helium filled mylar balloon, which is attached to a red, mylar mini gift bag balloon weight, on the end of the table Gina sits at as he sets up the cafeteria for lunch. Mark Gina's table with a large, yellow die cut number affixed to the table with clear contact paper (so that it can be easily wiped down).	___AT/Tech ___Career Ed. ___Comp./Access ___Ind. Liv. Skills ✓ O & M ___Rec./Leisure ✓ Self-Det. ✓ Sensory Eff. ___Soc. Inter.
-Rather than using a birdie that is white, which doesn't stand out against the surrounding white gymnasium walls, use a birdie that is fluorescent orange. Move Gina to a place near the net where the light shining through the window doesn't cause glare. Allow Gina to be on the left side of the court to better use her right visual field. -Make sure the science teacher is using fresh, black markers to write on a clean, dry erase board. Using the camera function on her iPad, allow Gina to walk up to the board to take a picture of the notes. Back at her desk, Gina can access the photo, zoom in, and save it for later use at home when completing the daily assignment. -Use the Acrobat 360 to locate the math problems then zoom in to see each problem individually (note; Gina only has one CCTV and except for testing and unusual circumstances, it stays in the Resource Room).	✓ AT/Tech ___Career Ed. ✓ Comp./Access ___Ind. Liv. Skills ___O & M ✓ Rec./Leisure ___Self-Det. ✓ Sensory Eff. ___Soc. Inter.
-Enlarge the map on a black and white photocopy machine. Gina does well with black and white line drawings so this may be easier for her. Simplify the maps by using correction fluid to take out non-essential details. Create more "white space" and reduce "visual clutter". -Busy pictures are often difficult for Gina. First, enlarge all pictures (same as above with maps). Then, highlight or outline the salient features in the pictures with a red Sharpie marker or a yellow highlighter.	___AT/Tech ___Career Ed. ✓ Comp./Access ___Ind. Liv. Skills ___O & M ___Rec./Leisure ___Self-Det. ✓ Sensory Eff. ___Soc. Inter.

© VeriNova, 2011-2016. All rights reserved.   StrategyToSee.com

CVI Strategy Areas		Has Skill (yes or no)	Activity(ies) that Strategy Area Impacts Observe student in one or more of the following areas to determine impact: Independent Living, Orientation and Mobility, Recreation/Leisure, Self-Determination, Sensory Efficiency, Social Interaction, Compensatory/Access, AT/Technology, Career Education, Fine/Gross Motor, PE, Speech and Language, and all areas of the Core Curriculum.
Spatial Window of Visual Attention and/or Viewing Array	Visually attends to one or two widely spaced visual target(s) at near (with good color contrast)	(yes)	
		no	
	Visually attends to 3-10 well spaced visual targets at near and/or distance (note distance and if SpotLighting, highlighting, or high contrast is needed)	(yes)	-During ELA when reading, Gina often loses her place on a line of print. -When completing math problems and using manipulatives, Gina often gets confused when too many manipulatives are in front of her. She especially misses counting or including the manipulatives that are on the desk on her left side.
		no	
	No difficulty attending to multiple targets at near and/or distance (no difficulty with "visual clutter" and/or poor contrast)	yes	
		(no)	
Contrast	Attends to near visual target(s) when presented against a solid colored background	(yes)	
		no	
	Attends to near visual target(s) when presented against multiple colors/patterns	(yes)	-When instructed to go and get something within the Resource Room setting (i.e. a stapler), Gina often is unable to locate it. -When a homework assignment is written on the board, Gina sometimes has a hard time finding where it is written (when sitting at her seat 10 feet away).
		no	
	Attends to visual target(s) in foreground and at distance with typical home/classroom "visual clutter" in background	yes	
		(no)	

© VeriNova, 2011-2016. All rights reserved.   StrategyToSee.com

Interventions, Strategies, and Recommendations Which Might Encourage More Efficient Use of Vision in this CVI Strategy Area	ECC Areas Addressed
-Encourage use of a pointer finger (Gina's) or window marker/Bright Line Marker to help keep place in a line of print. Download DAISY, Word and ePub books on to Gina's iPad and use the app Voice Dream, a text to speech app. Voice Dream allows a highly configurable screen layout, blocking all print above and below the line being read as well as the ability to yellow highlight each word as it is read. The text size, font, color and spacing are also fully customizable. Gina can use the app so that reading materials are completely auditory or completely visual or a combination of both. -Limit the number of manipulatives used and spread out what is being used. Encourage Gina to look at her far left and use scanning techniques. Present manipulatives on the CCTV XY table and enlarge so they can be viewed on the monitor. Use the contrast color feature to make the manipulatives stand out.	✓ AT/Tech ___ Career Ed. ✓ Comp./Access ___ Ind. Liv. Skills ___ O & M ___ Rec./Leisure ___ Self-Det. ✓ Sensory Eff. ___ Soc. Inter.
-Use directional/descriptive words when Gina needs to visually locate something in a "cluttered" classroom. For example, when asked to go and get a stapler, the teacher might say, "The black stapler is on my desk next to the colorful red and pink flowers". -Use a large sheet of yellow acetate (similar to the yellow vinyl sheet found in the APH Light Box Level I Materials) and trim it with red duct tape (1/2 inch in on all edges). Place this over the black printed Homework Assignment and attach to the dry erase board with a heavy-duty magnet. This will make the homework section on a "visually cluttered" dry erase board easier to locate.	___ AT/Tech ___ Career Ed. ___ Comp./Access ___ Ind. Liv. Skills ✓ O & M ___ Rec./Leisure ___ Self-Det. ✓ Sensory Eff. ___ Soc. Inter.

CVI Strategy Areas		Has Skill (yes or no)	Activity(ies) that Strategy Area Impacts Observe student in one or more of the following areas to determine impact: Independent Living, Orientation and Mobility, Recreation/Leisure, Self-Determination, Sensory Efficiency, Social Interaction, Compensatory/Access, AT/Technology, Career Education, Fine/Gross Motor, PE, Speech and Language, and all areas of the Core Curriculum.
Preferred Visual Field	Attends to visual target(s) at far left and/or far right visual field, approximately eye height at near	(yes) / no	
	Attends to visual target(s) in far left, far right, and/or central visual fields (limited or no attending lower visual field)	(yes) / no	-Gina still has difficulty with use of her lower visual field. When running both in the gym or out on the field during PE, Gina often trips over divots or items on the gym floor. She also often has difficulty following the running pattern while in the gym. -When working on printing in ELA, Gina often doesn't start at the far left of her paper. Each sentence printed moves progressively further right.
	Attends to visual target(s) in all visual fields including lower visual field	yes / (no)	
Lighting	Visually attracted to light; stares or stared at light source (i.e. sunlight or electric light)	(yes) / no	
	Visually attracted to light (or reflective targets) but can be redirected to other visual targets	(yes) / no	-Gina is no longer distracted by light or sunlight; however, she still seems to benefit from increased illumination on near materials. When working on worksheets, her body placement often causes a shadow over the worksheet and Gina often gets very close to the materials. This is partly due to her desire to reduce visual complexity, but when targets are spotLIGHTed, she is able to move further away.
	Visually attends to lights and non-lighted visual targets equally well. No staring at light sources noted	(yes) / no	
Familiarity	Attends to very familiar visual target(s) or target(s) student has looked at over and over	(yes) / no	
	Will look at target(s) that have been adapted with a quality that is favored or familiar (i.e. reflective mylar attached)	(yes) / no	-Gina continues to have difficulty with worksheets and paperwork with lots of print, symbols and visual clutter. She clearly has a target preference and that is when targets are simple, widely spaced and free from visual clutter.
	No target preference; attends to all targets, familiar and unfamiliar, equally well	yes / (no)	

© VeriNova, 2011-2016. All rights reserved.   StrategyToSee.com

Interventions, Strategies, and Recommendations Which Might Encourage More Efficient Use of Vision in this CVI Strategy Area	ECC Areas Addressed
-During PE when the students are running on the field, make sure that Gina uses the Buddy Technique and have a friend run along side of Gina with upper arms touching, giving both tactual and verbal cues as divots or bumps approach. Use of yellow tinted glasses might help to make divots stand out (ask optometrist about this). Remind Gina to look down and use scanning techniques often. Mark divots and bumps with small red flags, when possible. In the gym, run red duct tape along the wall at eye height and mark turns with lighted, safety cones. -Mark the left edge of the writing paper with a yellow highlighter and encourage Gina to start each sentence "In the yellow". Practice writing spelling words on an iPad using apps such as Light Box (Light Box HD by Amy Faulkner) and Glow Draw.	✓ AT/Tech ___ Career Ed. ___ Comp./Access ___ Ind. Liv. Skills ✓ O & M ___ Rec./Leisure ___ Self-Det. ✓ Sensory Eff. ___ Soc. Inter.
-When a supplementary light (or desk light) shines on worksheets and other near materials, it helps Gina to focus her visual attention on the spotlighted target and she is able to move further away from the materials. Use of the CCTV and the iPad are also helpful because of the backlighting feature both provide.	✓ AT/Tech ___ Career Ed. ✓ Comp./Access ___ Ind. Liv. Skills ___ O & M ___ Rec./Leisure ___ Self-Det. ✓ Sensory Eff. ___ Soc. Inter.
-Gina often benefits from color-coding, highlighted salient features, enlarged materials (creating more "white space"), use of correction fluid to take out non-essential information, use of window markers, and use of blocking techniques. When worksheets and printed materials are modified, even simply modified (i.e. use of yellow highlighter marking the answer lines on a worksheet), she is more confident and less stressed.	___ AT/Tech ___ Career Ed. ___ Comp./Access ___ Ind. Liv. Skills ___ O & M ___ Rec./Leisure ___ Self-Det. ✓ Sensory Eff. ___ Soc. Inter.

Additional Areas to Consider

Visual Fatigue

1. Does this student experience visual fatigue? Signs of visual fatigue may include, but not be limited to, yawning, fading attention, irritability, sleepiness, and crying.
Occasionally

2. Describe conditions in which visual fatigue occurs.
Gina will experience visual fatigue after reading for a long period of time or if ill or stressed.

3. How long is this student able to use their vision efficiently before visual fatigue occurs?
When working on reading for 30 - 45 minutes.

4. Certain ocular conditions cause visual fatigue including astigmatism. Does this student have an ocular condition (in addition to CVI), which may cause visual fatigue?
No, this student does not have an ocular condition that might cause visual fatigue.

5. What modifications or accommodations help to reduce visual fatigue?
It helps Gina to take frequent breaks, use apps when reading (like Voice Dream), and to have modified worksheets (large amounts of white space, color coding, enlarged, etc.)

Positioning

1. What is the best position for this student to be in while using vision? Consider meeting with the physical therapist, who can often give valuable advice on the best position for your student.
Gina works best when sitting at a desk and using a reading stand or slant board for reading materials.

2. Which position allows this student to use his/her arms most efficiently? For example, it might be leaning forward over a round bolster cushion.
N/A

3. Is there a specific chair and/or table/tray that works best with this student?
N/A

4. Do overhead lights or window light need to be considered when positioning this student? Will the position of the student cause a shadow on materials to be viewed?
Gina benefits from increased lighting on near materials, therefore, provide an additional supplementary light source and insure that it is positioned so no shadows are on the materials.

Eye/Hand Use

1. Is this student able to use his/her arms/hands to reach for objects?
Yes.

2. Does this student look at a target, then while looking at it, reach for or grasp the target (i.e. look and touch occur simultaneously)?
Yes, look and touch occur simultaneously.

3. Does this student look at a target, then look away and reach for or grasp the target (i.e. look and touch do not occur simultaneously)?
No.

4. What modifications will encourage look and touch to occur simultaneously? Consider reducing multi-sensory input, limiting number of targets, creating high contrast between target and background, SpotLighting target, and placement of target.
N/A

Notes

Chapter 10 - The PLAAFP and IEP Goals and Objectives

The PLAAFP

The PLAAFP is a special education acronym that stands for;

Present

Levels of

Academic

Achievement &

Functional

Performance

You may also see it called, **PLOP – P**resent **L**evel **O**f **P**erformance

The PLAAFP should provide information on where the student is currently performing in academic (if applicable) and functional skills (if applicable). This information allows the ARD Committee or IEP Committee to determine both an area of need and what the student can reasonably be expected to achieve within one year.

There are several places where you can find good information to help you develop your Present Level Statement for a student who is Cortically Visually Impaired, including;

- CVI Skills Inventory & Strategies Worksheet
- CVI Range
- Photographs
- Videotape
- Behavioral data
- Parent communication and interviews
- Teacher interviews
- Teacher made tests
- Skills Inventories (such as The Oregon Project)

The following is an example of General Information and PLAAFP excerpts for our student Amy (visually functioning in Phase I on the CVI Range), who was described in the Sample CVI Skills Inventory & Strategies Worksheet previously.

Amy has a history of premature birth, hydrocephalus, IVH - Grade IV, and seizures. Amy currently makes a variety of sounds, including gurgling, laughing, and single syllable sounds. While Amy has a diagnosis of a mild hearing loss bilaterally, she attends well to auditory stimuli and her parents' voices. She is currently non-mobile but working on sitting unaided. She is a happy little girl who expresses her pleasure by laughing. *Amy looks towards the window when sunlight is streaming through, and can briefly track a single moving target, such as a red, mylar pom pom when it is highlighted by a supplementary light (SpotLIGHTing). Amy also attends to a slow moving slinky when SpotLIGHTed. Amy does not attend to visual targets at mid-range or in the distance. Amy seems to use her right eye and far right visual field more consistently than her left. Amy is visually functioning in Phase I (1.50) on The CVI Range, Building Visual Behaviors.*

The PLAAFP (in italics highlighted in grey) links to Amy's annual Goal later in this chapter.

The following is an example of General Information and PLAAFP excerpts for our student Will (visually functioning in Phase II on the CVI Range), who was described in the Sample CVI Skills Inventory & Strategies Worksheet previously.

Will was born full term and at this time, while there are limited records regarding his birth, it is believed there were complications due to anoxia soon after he was born. Will has a medical diagnosis of Cerebral Palsy and his ophthalmologist has noted optic atrophy, nystagmus and Cortical Visual Impairment. Will is non-mobile and uses a wheel chair. He has limited use of his right hand/arm and generally uses his left hand for feeding and limited grasping. Will has no problems with his hearing and a recent screening noted, "hearing within normal limits for both ears". Will demonstrates good visual attending behavior to single colored targets, especially bright, highly saturated colored targets (red and yellow) when presented at near (less than 24 inches away). Will seems to use his vision more efficiently when near targets are well lit or SpotLIGHTed, raised up into his upper visual field, as on a slant board, and when they are presented against a solid, contrasting colored background. *Will seems to have more difficulty when asked to view multiple targets in a busy array and distance targets, especially when the distance target is embedded in a great deal of "visual clutter". With regard to pictures, Will seems to have more success with identification of pictures if they are a color photo of a single, real, common-to-him item. For example, a picture of his favorite solid colored ball presented against a solid colored background (i.e. black). When a color photo has a great deal of detail and other "visual clutter" in the photo, Will is less consistent with identification.* Will is visually functioning in Phase II on The CVI Range.

The PLAAFP (in italics highlighted in grey) links to Will's annual Goal later in this chapter.

The following is an example of General Information and PLAAFP excerpts for our student Gina (visually functioning in Phase III on the CVI Range), who was described in the Sample CVI Skills Inventory & Strategies Worksheet previously.

Gina enjoys playing a variety of iPad apps, especially those with music. She enjoys educational games, songs, and rhymes. She is able to write her numbers from 0-10, add and subtract single digit numbers, and count to 100. *Gina struggles with reading and writing. She is easily distracted and is only able to visually attend to educational materials for 15 minutes at a time. Gina reads 17 words per minute from a primmer level reader. She benefits from use of a line marker/window marker, a bookstand, and supplementary lighting. Recently, with use of an iPad (Book Creator, iBooks, and Pictello) in conjunction with her primmer reading program, Gina read 24 words per minute with increased comprehension. Her attention span has been greatly increased; she is currently able to sit in a quiet environment, reading for up to 20 minutes.* Gina's parents are reporting that she is now reading for enjoyment at home. Gina demonstrates functional vision in Phase III on The CVI Range.

The PLAAFP (in italics highlighted in grey) links to Gina's annual Goal later in this chapter.

Development of IEP Goals and Objectives

General guidelines for development of IEP Goals and Objectives can be offered but it is important to remember that children with CVI must be evaluated for his or her unique needs and behavior patterns.

General guidelines include the following;

Tie Goals and Objectives into all areas of the Expanded Core Curriculum.

Tie Goals and Objectives into skills targeted in the child's daily routines using the SLK Program.

Tie Goals and Objectives into activities that occur daily at home and at school. Remember, it is beneficial when activities relate to some functional purpose.

Tie Goals and Objectives to the 10 Behavioral Characteristics of the CVI Range (see the IEP Development Guide in the book, *Cortical Visual Impairment; An Approach to Assessment and Intervention*).

Tie Goals and Objectives to strategies and interventions noted on the completed CVI Skills Inventory & Strategies Worksheet for your student.

Write Goals and Objectives together with the classroom teacher or Learning Partner (Integrated Direct).

Measurable Goal and Short-term Objective with a Timeframe, Condition(s), Behavior and Criterion

Timeframe; The Timeframe identifies the amount of time in the Goal/Objective period.

- In 36 instructional weeks...
- By the end of the 2012-2013 school year..
- By May 28, 2013...
- During the first 9 week period...
- During the second 9 week period...
- During the third 9 week period...
- By the end of the 4th 9 week period...

Condition(s); A Condition describes the manner in which progress toward the goal/objective occurs. It also describes specific resources and materials.

- Using a black Invisiboard, a red slinky, and a bright light,.....
- When given a blinking, bright red spoon on a black placemat,....
- When provided a modified Elmo book with a single picture on each page and asked, "Touch Elmo",

Behavior; A Behavior clearly identifies the performance that is being monitored. It can be an action that can be directly observed and measured.

- Annie, a 3-year old toddler, will visually alert to and track the movement of the (slinky)....
- Sam, a 2- year old little boy, will visually locate then reach out and grasp the (spoon)....
- Pam, a 2nd grade student, will visually locate (Elmo) and touch the picture of (Elmo)......

Criterion; Criterion identifies how much, how often, or to what standard the behavior must occur in order to demonstrate that the goal/objective has been achieved.

- in 3 out of 5 trials
- at least 4 out of 5 times, 2 times per day
- with no more than one gestural prompt in 3 out of 5 tries

An example of a Goal for a student who benefits from Level 1 Strategies, like our sample student **Amy**, might be;

In 36 instructional weeks, using a high powered flashlight, red and yellow lighted targets, red and yellow slinky, red mylar pom pom, APH Light Box, Invisiboard, All-In-One Board, Philips LightAide, tablet technology and black sheeting, Amy, a preschool student, will increase sensory efficiency skills by visually tracking a target and reaching for a near target 4 out of 5 presentations. "Visually tracking" will include following the movement of a near (within 18 inches) target moving from student's far right visual field to at least midline. "Reaching for a near target" will include movement of one or both hands in the direction of the target and/or grasping the target.

Short Term Objectives might be;

1. By the end of the first 9 weeks, using a high powered flashlight, red and yellow lighted targets, red and yellow slinky, red mylar pom pom, APH Light Box, Invisiboard, All-In-One Board, Philips LightAide, tablet technology and black sheeting, Amy will visually alert to a single colored or lighted target, presented in the far right visual field, during 4 out of 5 presentations with a tactual cue. "Visually alert to" may include, but not be limited to, looking in the direction of the visual target, opening eyes larger when the visual target is presented and/or vocalization when the target is presented.

2. By the end of the second 9 weeks, using a high powered flashlight, red and yellow lighted targets, red and yellow slinky, red mylar pom pom, APH Light Box, Invisiboard, All-In-One Board, Philips LightAide, tablet technology and black sheeting, Amy will visually track a moving single colored or lighted target when presented in the far right visual field and moved toward the central visual field in 4 out of 5 presentations with an auditory cue.

3. By the end of the third 9 weeks, using a high powered flashlight, red and yellow lighted targets, red and yellow slinky, red mylar pom pom, APH Light Box, Invisiboard, All-In-One Board, Philips LightAide, tablet technology and black sheeting, Amy will demonstrate reaching behavior towards a target with one or both hands in 4 out of 5 presentations with an auditory cue. "Reaching behavior" may include, but not be limited to, a slight lift of one hand or movement of a hand and arm in response to the presentation of the target. Note; student may turn head away from target when using reaching behavior.

4. By the end of the fourth 9 weeks, using a high powered flashlight, red and yellow lighted targets, red and yellow slinky, red mylar pom pom, APH Light Box, Invisiboard, All-In-One Board, Philips LightAide, tablet technology and black sheeting, Amy will demonstrate reaching and grasping behavior in response to the presentation of a visual target in her near visual field, in 4 out of 5 presentations. Note; student may still benefit

from touch and/or auditory cues and may turn head away from target when using reaching/grasping behavior.

An example of a Goal and Objectives for a student who benefits from Level 2 Strategies, like our sample student **Will**, might be;

By the end of the 2014 – 2015 school year, using a black Velcro compatible Daily Calendar with "Now" and "Next" columns, 18 photos of familiar daily items mounted on black foam core (Velcro on the back), an Invisiboard and a red "Finished Basket", Will, an elementary school student, will increase Compensatory Skills by placing the photo of the activity just completed in the "Finished Basket", moving the photo that was in the "Next" spot to the "Now" spot and locating a teacher specified new photo (activity) to place in the "Next" spot, at least 4 out of 5 times correctly during a school day. Note; the 18 photos of familiar daily items all represent activities that Will is involved in throughout the day, such as recess, daily circle time, ELA, etc.

Short Term Objectives might be;

1. By the end of the first 9 weeks, using a black Velcro compatible Daily Calendar with "Now" and "Next" columns, 18 photos of familiar daily items mounted on black foam core (Velcro on the back) and an Invisiboard, Will, an elementary school student, will increase Compensatory Skills by locating a requested photo when given a choice of 2 (well-spaced photos) and place it on the calendar under the word "Now", at least 4 out of 5 times correctly during a school day. Note; this will be done before each activity throughout the day, with the photo that represents that activity.

2. By the end of the second 9 weeks, using a black Velcro compatible Daily Calendar with "Now" and "Next" columns, 18 photos of familiar daily items mounted on black foam core (Velcro on the back) and an Invisiboard, Will, an elementary school student, will increase Compensatory Skills by locating a requested photo when given a choice of 5 (well-spaced photos) and place it on the calendar under the word "Now", at least 4 out of 5 times correctly during a school day. Note; this will be done before each activity throughout the day, with the photo that represents that activity.

3. By the end of the third 9 weeks, using a black Velcro compatible Daily Calendar with "Now" and "Next" columns, 18 photos of familiar daily items mounted on black foam core (Velcro on the back), an Invisiboard and a red "Finished Basket", Will, an elementary school student, will increase Compensatory Skills by locating a requested photo (when given a choice of 5) and place it on the calendar under the word "Now" (before the activity begins), and then after the activity is finished, remove the photo from the "Now" column and put it in the "Finished Basket", at least 4 out of 5 times correctly during a school day.

4. By the end of the fourth 9 weeks, using a black Velcro compatible Daily Calendar with "Now" and "Next" columns, 18 photos of familiar daily items mounted on black foam core (Velcro on the back), an Invisiboard and a red "Finished Basket", Will, an elementary school student, will increase Compensatory Skills by removing the photo from the "Now" column of the calendar and placing it in the "Finished Basket" (once the activity is finished) and then moving the photo from the "Next" column to the "Now" column, at least 4 out of 5 times correctly during a school day.

An example of a Goal and Objectives for a student who benefits from Level 3 Strategies, like our sample student **Gina**, might be;

In 36 Instructional weeks, given direct instruction using a tablet, VoiceDream (app), an uploaded primmer level passage, a reading stand, a study carrel and guided practice, Gina will increase technology skills by accessing a teacher selected book in VoiceDream, set 1 line visible, set text size (67), set highlighting on text and orally read 28 words per minute with 6 or fewer errors. Note; the text-to-speech function will be turned off.

Short Term Objectives might be;

1. Within the first 18-week period, given direct instruction using a tablet, VoiceDream (app), headphones, an uploaded primmer level passage, a reading stand, a study carrel and guided practice, Gina will increase technology skills by accessing the VoiceDream app, locating a teacher selected book, accessing the visual settings (adjust the text size) and with no more than 2 verbal prompts, will orally read 25 words per minute with 5 or fewer errors.

2. Within the second 18-week period, given direct instruction using a tablet, VoiceDream (app), headphones, an uploaded primmer level passage, a reading stand, a study carrel and guided practice, Gina will increase technology skills by accessing a teacher selected book, access the visual settings (adjust text size and lines visible) and with no more than 1 verbal prompt, will orally read 26 words per minute with 6 or fewer errors.

Chapter 11 - Strategies for Improving Literacy Skills in Students with CVI

Literacy, the ability to <u>read</u> for knowledge, <u>write</u> coherently, and <u>think</u> critically about the written word, is a skill we hope every child will achieve. Students with CVI, particularly those who visually function in Phase III of The CVI Range, are using interesting strategies to achieve their beginning reading goals. I would like to share some of these strategies and others I have found helpful to students I work with. My hope is that you will use these suggestions and ideas to further literacy in children you too work with who have Cortical Visual Impairment.

This chapter will be divided into two parts; Strategies for Pre-Readers and Strategies for Beginning Readers. Some students who visually function towards the high end of Phase II may benefit from some of the ideas for Pre-Readers, but generally, students who visually function in Phase III will benefit most from these strategies.

Strategies for Pre-Readers

Before beginning any formal reading program, you will need to make sure your student or child has mastered many pre-reading skills. These vary, depending on which literacy program you explore, but generally they include most of the following;

Print Motivation; This may be one of the most important pre-reading skills to consider. Make sure that reading time is fun. Use strategies outlined in this chapter to ensure that books are "CVI Friendly". Keep reading time short, but do it often. Create books that are predictable, with something recognizable appearing on every page. For example, if your child has an Elmo doll and easily recognizes this stuffed toy, create CVI Friendly books with Elmo as the main character. If your child has a particular brightly colored ball he loves and easily recognizes, create a book using this familiar toy. Use tablet technology to create custom books of high interest to the child. The app Pictello is what I use often to create my own books. You may find that books with reflective, mylar-like pages are interesting to your child or books with only a single, red object on each page is motivating. Don't forget to SpotLIGHT the individual pages, if this works for your child. You may need to search or do some work in this area, but print motivation is very important.

Making "CVI Friendly" books can be easy and fun. I have found that black, Pro Click Binding Covers (and Pro Click Spines) work well. Remember to use the non-shiny side of the cover (the other side creates glare). You can use the entire page (8 ½ inches by 11 inches) or cut them in half. Remember to use mat finish photos of your student's familiar, well loved, toys and objects. These pictures can also be uploaded into programs such as Pictello. See Creating "CVI Friendly" Books, at the end of this chapter for more information.

Direction; Having an understanding that print goes from left to right will be important as are concepts like top, bottom, front and back. Although your child may not understand these directional concepts, use them often as you work with books.

Motor Skills; Getting your student to be interested in and help with page turning is made more doable when you use "Page Fluffers" or spacers. Small fingers have an easier time helping to turn a page when there is a space between pages. Most Page Fluffers are placed on the upper right corner of each page. A Page Fluffer can be as simple as using a drop of glue from a hot glue gun (made as thick or as thin as you want) or a clear, silicone bumper (the type you use on the bottom of a vase). Alternately, you can use squares of adhesive backed Velcro, squares of adhesive backed weather stripping, adhesive backed felt circles (used on the feet of furniture), small squares of foam core (glued directly on to each page) or even staggered paper clips.

A good book to use to practice page turning for a student who visually functions in Phase II or Phase III would be, "My First Book of Symbols" and, "My Second Book of Symbols". Both books are CVI Friendly and developed by Dr. Marva Gelhaus and the South Dakota Foundation for the Blind and Visually Impaired. See the Resources section of this book for ordering details.

When using electronic books on a tablet, often there is the small triangle one needs to touch to move to the next page. These can be difficult for the student with CVI to locate. Try using a Fling Game Controller (Ten One Design) modified on top with a red, mylar-like dot. Place a Fling on top of the triangle, and it makes locating the page turning function easier.

Print Awareness; Students need to understand that print on a page represents words that are spoken. They also need to learn to hold a book and to follow words on a page. Use photos of favorite, familiar items and create a "CVI Friendly" book with them. Add one word per page and discuss the salient features of the letters and the shape of the word. Use a red Sharpie marker to draw attention to a specific feature (i.e. the E in Elmo might be outlined in red and discuss that it is like a table turned sideways but with only 3 legs, etc.).

Rhyming and Phonological Awareness; Students will need to understand that words are all made up of smaller sounds. Create electronic books (with Pictello) using favored targets and rhyming words. For example, if your student loves Elmo, create a book with the "at" family of words; Elmo Sat, Elmo's Hat, Elmo's Cat, etc. Each page can show

Elmo with the item or doing the action. Use a good search engine such as Bing (Bing for iPad) to help you locate specific images.

Letter Knowledge; Students will need to know that each letter is different from others. They will need to be able to recognize and name all letters and know that each has a different sound. Using red foam letters, allow students to sort using an APH yellow sorting tray, outlined in red duct tape. To begin with, use only three letters, two being the same, and gradually add more letters to sort as you discuss their names.

Matching; Students with CVI will need experience in matching shapes, letters and numbers. They will need to understand the concepts, "same" and "different". Use a variety of items when teaching sorting of same and different, but make sure they are appropriate to the level of visual functioning of the student. For example, use large red buttons and large yellow buttons spread out on a black, Velcro compatible mat (as discussed earlier). Sorting bowls could be in a bright color as well. Use an APH Light Box with two colors of translucent bowls and two colors of cubes to sort and match.

Narrative Skills; Students with CVI will need experience in telling and understanding stories. They need to describe things and events. Use an All-In-One Board and attach favored, familiar items (with Velcro on the back) and create a story. The slant of the All-In-One Board brings the targets into the field of view and the black background helps to reduce visual clutter and create contrast. Let the student make up a story using their familiar items as well. Alternately, use brightly colored window clings on a Light Box to help tell a story or spark a discussion.

Vocabulary; It will be important for students to know the names of things, feelings, concepts and ideas. Label common, everyday objects the student comes in contact with. Make name labels by using a black, bold marker on pre-cut pieces of yellow tag board. Discuss the salient features of all objects. Discuss the salient features of letters and words. For example, if the child's door is labeled, you could talk about how the word "Door" has two circles in the middle that look like two eyes. Discuss the overall shape of the word "Door". Point out words the student comes in contact with during naturally occurring routines.

Strategies for Beginning Readers

Once pre-reading skills are mastered a formal reading program can be considered or introduced. Students who use Level 3 Strategies presented in Chapter 7 often benefit from these suggestions.

Use the most current Functional Vision Evaluation to determine;
    The most appropriate font (usually, a simple font like Arial or APHont works well)
    The most appropriate print size (a good starting point might be 24pt.)

Placement of the materials (left, right, flat, on bookstand, etc.)
Use of supplementary lighting, SpotLIGHTing, or backlighting
Use of blocking materials to limit complexity

The use of blocking materials will vary depending on need. Blocking materials help to block out excess detail on a page of print, images or symbols. Blocking materials include;
Window cards or window markers
A sheet of black construction paper
Markers or Bright Line Markers from APH
Templates

When possible, create more "White Space" or reduce the information on a page of print.
Use correction fluid
Physically cut out excess print and paste on more white paper
Block off excess print with white paper and photocopy the new, simplified version
Enlarge on a photocopy machine
Choose materials that offer reduced "clutter" and more "white space"
Discuss with ophthalmologist or optometrist the possibility of using reading glasses (+lens)
Fold the page

Determine the type of picture your student is best able to visually interpret.
Pictures of Real (especially familiar) Targets – This is best accomplished with a color photograph of a single, brightly colored target presented against a black background. You have to be very careful that only the target of interest is photographed. If there is too much clutter around and behind the target of interest, the target will get lost.

Black and white illustrations - I have had the most success with **simple**, black and white illustrations, with a key feature (or two) highlighted on each page, keeping it the same throughout the book. I often use a yellow highlighter or outline with a permanent ultra-fine point red pen.

Color illustrations - Many times, these are just too complex and cartoon-like for the child with CVI to interpret. Check carefully to make sure the child can correctly identify these.

Use permanent markers and highlighters to draw visual attention to a specific, key feature (or features). Use this technique consistently throughout the book.

Highlight a key feature (or two) in a picture (as noted above)
Highlight new words
Highlight high frequency words
Highlight salient features of a word
Let the student visually locate and highlight new words in a passage or book

Choose an appropriate literacy program.
The Primary Phonics Series (by Barbara W. Makar) Sets 1-10 is one of my favorites. This program can be ordered through Amazon. The series has simple black and white line drawn illustrations, lots of "white space", is easy to use with tablet programs such as Book Creator and VoiceDream but it is sometimes difficult to locate the books. The Wilson Reading System has also been successful for some TVIs.

Use PowerPoint Presentations and Smart Boards in conjunction with your student's literacy program.

Consider the use of "cheat sheets", mnemonic devices and guides to help during lessons.

Always reduce or eliminate distracting sensory input.
Reduce or eliminate unnecessary auditory input, including outdoor noises, whenever possible.
Reduce or eliminate unnecessary tactual input.
Reduce or eliminate unnecessary visual input, including flashy jewelry the teacher might be wearing.

SLOW down!
Give your student time to think about the word(s).
Give your student time to remember key points.
Give your student time to recall mnemonic devices.
Give your student time to process the information.

Use Tablet Technology and Apps in conjunction with your reading program.

Book Creator can be used to support and provide practice, highlight salient features of words, highlight phonetic rules, and present mnemonic devices for any program you are using. You use this application in conjunction with iBooks.

Pictello is a simple way to create talking photo albums and talking books on your tablet. You can record your own voice or use text to speech. You can import your own photos or use photos from the Internet. You can control the speech rate and volume.

Voice Dream is a text to speech app, which reads PDF, ePub, DAISY, Word and other text files and downloaded books (Bookshare). You can use completely auditory, completely visual or a combination of both. You can black out sentences above and below the line being read and then highlight in yellow each word as it is being read. Text size, font, color and spacing are fully adjustable.

Light Box HD, by Amy Faulkner can be used to practice writing new vocabulary words (it is free). Use the blank, light-box-like screen and choose the red paint spatter (or the student's preferred color) and practice writing letters, words and more.

SnapType (for Occupational Therapists) can be used to help students' complete worksheets by taking a picture then typing on them.

Creating "CVI Friendly" Books

Children who have a diagnosis of Cortical Visual Impairment, or have some form of brain damage related vision loss, have distinct needs when it comes to literacy exposure and experiences. There are very few commercial books on the market that meet these needs, but by following a few guidelines, "CVI Friendly" books can be created at home or in the classroom setting. When children are learning to use their vision for functional purposes, pre-reading skills can be worked on with custom made books. As students learn to use their vision more consistently and efficiently, there are many strategies that could be used to develop important literary concepts and by creating your own books, individual needs can be met.

Guidelines for creating CVI Friendly books

- Use flat black (non-glossy) heavy paper for the pages. Pro-Click makes a product, which provides "*Spines* and *Covers*" in black. The spines and covers can be cut to size. The covers are pre-punched to accommodate the spines. This product can be found in most office supply stores.

- Use black spines or binders that can be easily opened and closed as needed (Pro-Click spines can do this). Sometimes you may want to only show one, or maybe two pages at a time, to give choices, and therefore want to click open the spine, take out a page or two, then re-close it.

- Make sure your choice of picture style is appropriate for the student. Does the student need color photos of real objects? Do black and white line drawings work better? Do color illustrations work best? The best rule of thumb may be to use color photos of only a single object, or person, against a solid contrasting color, such as black. Use a matte finish on the photos, which will reduce glare and fingerprints.

- Use clear, rubber Bumpers (sold at hardware stores) at the top, right corner of each page, to help separate the pages (see other Page Fluffer suggestions noted previously). This encourages turning the page independently by little fingers and helps with fine motor skills. (NOTE: Bumpers are often used as "little protective feet" under a vase or used on the back of a frame hanging on a wall, so it won't mar the wall).

- For students who benefit from Level 2 Strategies, use only one item or person in the picture per page. For students who benefit from Level 3 Strategies, two or three items or people can be in the picture, but the picture may still need to be simple (low in complexity and detail).

- When making a book of familiar people (mom, dad, siblings, grandparents, etc.) photograph the person against a solid colored wall (no wall hangings), the upper body of the person and make sure the person is wearing a solid colored shirt. The person's face should stand out with limited complexity around it. Note; identification of people in photos is often difficult, even for students who use Level 3 Strategies.

- When words are added to pages, make sure the font is simple and bold. Use of Ariel or APHont (by APH) works well. Remember to emphasize salient features of letters and words.

- When words are added to the pages, make sure the font size is appropriate. I find that 24pt. font works well. You may find that double spacing between words and using double line spacing between sentences also helps to create less "visual clutter".

- When possible, let the student help choose the topic of the book.

- Make custom books using Tablet applications such as Pictello, Book Creator and iBooks. Use Bing Search to locate specific pictures on the Internet when creating your books. For example, if you are working on the Word Family "at" and want to have pictures representing "at" words, you might search for pictures such as Elmo with a Cat (Elmo's Cat), Elmo with a Hat (Elmo's Hat), and Elmo with a Bat (Elmo's Bat), using Bing (Bing for iPad)

- When your student is ready to have print added to their books, start off with one word to represent the photo or picture on the page. For example if the picture is of Elmo, you might simply add the word, "Elmo" below the picture. When the student is ready for more print, describe the visual target(s) in terms of its salient features. For example, if the target is a favorite ball, you might say, "This is an Oball. The shape is round and the color is orange. When you shake it, it makes a sound like rain coming down." This same concept can be used when creating books on your tablet using iBooks, PowerPoint, Pictello or Book Creator.

Suggested books to make for the child who benefits from Level 2 or Level 3 Strategies

Time to Eat Book would include not only familiar, favorite foods the child enjoys, but also familiar mealtime utensils, bowls and cups. If the child enjoys bananas, you could photograph a bright yellow banana placed against a solid, black background. If the child used a favorite sippy cup every day, photograph it alone against a solid contrasting color background.

Favorite Toys Book might include all of the familiar, favored "toys" the child plays with or interacts with. This might include pictures of unique "toys" or favored items the child loves, such as a mylar-like gift bag, a reflective silver pie tin or a cell phone. The photograph should be of one "toy" only. When photographing the "toy", present it against a solid colored, contrasting background.

Alphabet Book would have 1 letter on each page with a picture of a familiar target to represent the letter. For example, the first page might be "A" and if your student loves apples, use a photograph of a red apple. For "B", you might have a picture of "Big Bird", if your student is familiar with the Sesame Street's big yellow bird.

Shape Book could focus on simple shapes such as circle, square and triangle. Cut the shapes out of reflective, bright red or yellow mylar-like paper. Use only one shape per page. Use heavy, black, non-glossy paper for the pages. Use SpotLIGHTing techniques to focus visual attention on the reflective shape.

Suggested books to make for the child who benefits from Level 3 Strategies

Experience Book might be about a daily routine that the child is familiar with, such as breakfast. Photograph real objects for the pictures on each page such as the child's familiar, red bowl, the favored cereal and the chair the child regularly sits in. A single word can be added below each photograph such as, "Cheerios".

Favorite People Book which shows one <u>familiar</u>, favorite person per page such as Mom, Dad, brother, sister, caretaker, teacher, grandma and/or grandpa. Make this suggested book only if your student has little or no difficulty with looking at and identifying a familiar face both in person and in a photo.

Chapter 12 - Forms

The following forms are provided to help with the completion process of the CVI Skills Inventory & Strategies Worksheet.

SpotLIGHTing Techniques

This handout on SpotLIGHTing Techniques can be copied and given to parents, teachers and others. These techniques can be used with students just beginning to use their vision since they are often attracted to lights and lighted targets. We can use this to our advantage by SpotLIGHTing a reflective target or object we might use for self-help. Students who are working towards resolving CVI Behavioral Characteristics and using their vision well may still benefit from extra light in their educational environment or light on a specific target of significance. This guide may be reproduced.

Interview Forms

Interviewing parents, caretakers, teachers and others who care for and work with students with CVI is essential in order to gain a full understanding of the functional vision that the student has and uses. To that end, two different forms are provided for interviewing parents and/or caretakers (one for students who benefit from Level 1 and 2 Strategies and one for students who benefit from Level 3 Strategies). A third form is provided to interview a Teacher, Paraprofessional, or Nurse of a Student with CVI. These forms may be reproduced.

SpotLIGHTing Techniques

The use of **SpotLIGHTing Techniques** should be considered for increasing visual attending behaviors for targets at near and intermediate ranges. This instructional strategy is simple and easy to use, and may help to increase visual attending behavior and the level of participation in activities for students who alert frequently to light. This technique should not be used if your student is sensitive to light and/or has a seizure disorder that may be triggered by light.

SpotLIGHTing involves the following:

- Use of a high powered flashlight with at least 300 lumens; 1,000 to 1,200 works best (do NOT shine this high powered flashlight into the student's eyes!)
- When a toy, target or other interesting visual item is presented to the student, shine the light onto the object
- Shine the light onto the target from behind the student (over his/her shoulder), so that the student is not turning to locate and look at the light source
- With smaller, high powered flashlights, try moving the flashlight to within inches of the object, illuminating only the object
- Avoid glare reflecting from the target
- Remember to present the SpotLIGHTed target in the student's best field of view (and within 36 inches for the child who benefits from Level 1 Strategies)
- At first, encourage the student to attend briefly to the lighted target (this process may need to be repeated often, in an environment that encourages looking behavior; reduce environmental complexity and as well as auditory and tactual interfering stimulation)
- Next, encourage the student to follow or track the movement of the target
- Finally, encourage the student to become involved in some way with the lighted target. This might include, but is not limited to, reaching out to touch the target, reaching to grasp the target, shaking the target or using it for some functional purpose (grasping a cup to take a drink)
- The end goal is that objects are presented without SpotLIGHTing and the student visually attends equally well, as the same looking behaviors are encouraged

Alternate SpotLIGHTing Technique;

For students working with books and other materials on white paper, try using a high-powered flashlight, SpotLIGHTing an individual letter or target from *behind* the paper. The flashlight illuminates the individual target of interest. Press the lighted end of the flashlight right onto the back of the page. The student looking at it from the other side sees the target of interest illuminated. Don't forget that some students benefit from increased illumination on near educational materials, as from a natural desk light.

INTERVIEW FORM – PARENT/CAREGIVER of a Student with CVI

(For students who are just beginning to use their vision or are starting to use it for functional purposes)

Parent/Caregiver's Name_____   Interviewer's Name_____

Student's Name _____   Date_____

1. What is the cause of your child's visual impairment, as you understand it?

2. What surgeries has your child had?

3. Tell me about any medication(s) your child currently takes and if you notice any visual side effect as a result of the medication(s).

4. When was your child's last visit to the ophthalmologist or optometrist? Does your child wear glasses?

5. Tell me about your child's birth and background medical history. Has your child had a CT scan or MRI? If so, was there anything significant regarding the results?

6. Does your child have any difficulties with hearing? Has your child had an ABR and what were the results?

7. Does your child have a history of seizures?

8. Does your child have a shunt?

9. Tell me about the program that your child is currently in (if any). Does your child receive PT, OT, Speech, or any other ongoing services?

10. What are your concerns about your child's vision?

11. When do you notice your child using his/her vision the most? In a quiet room where there are no auditory distractions? Does tactual interaction cause your child to use his/her vision more or less (i.e. rubbing of the back, bouncing, etc.)?

12. When your child uses his/her vision to attend to an object, at what distance is that object from his/her face?

13. Tell me about the visual targets or toys that your child will look at. What is his/her favorite visual target? Is there a specific color he/she will attend to more than another? Tell me about how the target is presented to your child (i.e. on a colorful baby blanket,

hanging from a baby gym, on a plain table, etc.). Note; a favorite visual target does not necessarily have to be a toy.

14. When your child looks at a visual target or targets, how many targets will he/she look at in an array? Is vision used more consistently when there is only one target in front of your child?

15. Do you notice that your child more often visually alerts to objects/toys when presented on one side more than the other? Does your child tilt or turn his/her head when visually observing a target? If mobile, does your child trip over objects in his/her lower visual field?

16. Will your child visually attend to your face (or recognize you) when there are no auditory/verbal or tactual cues. If so, how far away are you from your child?

17. Is your child attracted to lights or sunny windows? Describe the setting/lighting if so. How far away are the lights/window, what color are the lights, and can your child's attention be redirected after he/she has been looking at lights/windows?

18. If given an unfamiliar toy or object, would your child respond to it or would he/she only respond to familiar toys/targets?

19. What position does your child feel most secure in? What is the best position for your child to be in while using his/her vision?

20. Are there any other concerns you have with regard to your child's vision that we have not discussed? Are there any specific settings that you would like me to see your child in?

NOTES:

INTERVIEW FORM – PARENT/CAREGIVER of a Student with CVI

(For students who are beginning to resolve CVI characteristics or who use their vision for pre-reading or academic purposes)

Parent/Caregiver's Name_____ Interviewer's Name_____

Student's Name _____ Date_____

1. What is the cause of your child's visual impairment, as you understand it?

2. What surgeries has your child had?

3. Tell me about any medication(s) your child currently takes and if you notice any visual side effect as a result of the medication(s).

4. When was your child's last visit to the ophthalmologist or optometrist? Does your child wear glasses? Has he/she had a Low Vision Evaluation? Use Low Vision Devices?

5. Tell me about your child's birth and background medical history. Has your child had a CT scan or MRI? If so, was there anything significant regarding the results?

6. Does your child have any difficulties with hearing? Has your child had an ABR and what were the results?

7. Does your child have a history of seizures?

8. Does your child have a shunt?

9. Tell me about the program that your child is currently in (if any). Does your child receive PT, OT, Speech or any other ongoing services?

10. What are your concerns about your child's use of vision? Tell me about routines or activities that your child has a hard time completing specifically because of difficulties with use of vision.

11. When do you notice your child using vision most consistently and efficiently?

12. When there are no auditory cues present, will your child attend to visual targets at 6 to 10 feet away? Up to 10 to 20 feet away? Give examples.

13. Tell me about the visual targets, books, pictures, worksheets, etc. that your child will look at. Tell me about the best arrangement for the target to be presented to your child (i.e. flat on a table, at an angle on a reading stand, etc.).

14. What high and low-tech devices does your child use on a regular basis? High and low-tech devices might include (but are not limited to) supplementary lighting, slant board, tablet, computer, modified keyboard, magnifier, hand held telescope and CCTV.

15. When your child looks at a visual target or targets, how many targets will he/she look at in an array? Is vision used more consistently when there is only one target in front of your child or can he/she look at many targets at once?

16. Do you notice that your child more often visually attends to objects when presented on one side more than the other? Does your child tilt or turn his/her head when visually observing a target? If/when mobile, does your child trip over objects when they are in the lower visual field?

17. Will your child visually attend to your face (or recognize you) when there are no auditory/verbal or tactual cues. If so, how far away are you from your child?

18. Is your child attracted to toys or objects that light up? If so, give examples. Does your child enjoy using a tablet? If so, what types of apps work well for your child?

19. What is the best position for your child to be in while using vision? Is his/her best position in an adapted chair, sitting in a standard chair at a table, in a wheelchair, etc.

20. Do you notice that your child gets visually fatigued? If so, what are the circumstances when you notice your child getting visually fatigued (i.e. when your child is ill, stressed, tired) and how does he/she demonstrate visual fatigue (i.e. fussy, closes eyes, etc.)?

21. Are there any other concerns you have with regard to your child's vision that we have not discussed? Are there any specific settings that you would like me to see your child in?

NOTES:

INTERVIEW FORM – TEACHER, PARAPROFESSIONAL OR NURSE OF A STUDENT with CVI

Teacher's Name_____ Interviewer's Name_____

Student's Name _____ Date_____

1. What is your understanding of this student's visual impairment?

2. What program is this student in? Other than vision, what other handicapping conditions does this student have?

3. What are this student's Special Education Eligibilities and which Support Services does he/she receive?

4. Do you have any concerns with regard to this student's hearing?

5. Does this student have a shunt or have seizures?

6. Does this student take any medication(s) and if so, do you notice any visual side effect as a result of the medication(s)?

7. At what time of the day is this student most alert, on the ball and ready to learn?

8. Describe this student's strengths?

9. Do you notice this student using his/her vision more in a room that is quiet, with no auditory distractions or is vision used consistently in a typical, multisensory environment, such as a preschool classroom?

10. When there is no auditory cue, what is the distance that this student is able to view objects at? Near only (up to 36 inches away)? Up to 6 or 10 feet away? Or will he/she attend to visual objects at 10 to 20 feet away (i.e. a large beach ball)?

11. Describe what type of visual targets this student will look at. Single colored targets (what color?), lighted targets, targets in 2-3 colors, simple black line pictures or photographs, books, worksheets, etc.

12. Describe the optimal viewing array for this student. Will this student only attend to one individual target in front of him/her at near? Can the student attend to several targets at once in front of him/her at near? Does the student benefit from high contrast behind the targets?

13. Will the student view multiple targets at distance, as on a dry erase board in a typical classroom? If so, what is the distance the multiple targets are at?

14. Do you notice that this student has a preferred visual field? For example, does he/she attend more frequently when a visual target is at one side more than the other? Does he/she attend to visual targets when they are lying flat on a table or tray? When

multiple targets are spread out in front of the student, does he/she consistently miss seeing targets at one side or the other? If the student is mobile, does he/she have difficulty seeing objects on the floor?

15. Is this student visually attracted to light (sunny windows, overhead lights)? Does this student look at toys and objects that light up? If so, can this student be redirected to other non-lighted targets?

16. Does this student only visually attend to specific, familiar visual targets or will he/she look at any target that is presented?

17. Does this student demonstrate visual fatigue? If so, under what circumstances does this happen (i.e. ill, stressed, tired, etc.)

18. Is there a specific position in which this student is better able to use his/her vision (i.e. sitting in a wheelchair, sitting in a modified chair, etc.)?

19. What high and low-tech devices does this student use on a regular basis in an educational setting? High and low-tech devices might include (but are not limited to) supplementary lighting, slant board, tablet, computer, modified keyboard, magnifier, hand held telescope and CCTV.

20. What is your favorite strategy that you use to get this student to use his/her vision most efficiently?

21. What are your concerns regarding this student's use of vision? Tell me about routines or activities that this student has a hard time completing specifically because of difficulties with use of vision.

22. Are there any other concerns you have with regard to this student's vision that we have not discussed? Are there any specific settings that you would like me to see this student in?

NOTES:

Resources

Books Recommended by the Author

Baniel, Anat. *Kids beyond Limits: The Anat Baniel Method for Awakening the Brain and Transforming the Life of Your Child with Special Needs.* New York, NY: Perigee Trade, 2012. Print.

Dodson-Burk, Bonnie, and Christine Roman. *Preschool Orientation and Mobility Screening.* Alexandria, VA.: Association for Education and Rehabilitation of the Blind and Visually Impaired, 2012. Print.

Doidge, Norman. *The Brain That Changes Itself: Stories of Personal Triumph from the Frontiers of Brain Science.* New York: Viking, 2007. Print.

Lueck, Amanda Hall. *Functional Vision: A Practitioner's Guide to Evaluation and Intervention.* New York, NY: American Foundation for the Blind, 2004. Print.

Lueck, Amanda Hall, and Gordon Dutton, *Vision and the Brain: Understanding Cerebral Visual Impairment in Children.* New York; AFB, 2015. Print

Nelson, Catherine. *Child-guided Strategies: The Van Dijk Approach to Assessment: For Understanding Children and Youth with Sensory Impairments and Multiple Disabilities.* Louisville: American Printing House for the Blind, 2009. Print

Roman-Lantzy, Christine. *Cortical Visual Impairment: An Approach to Assessment and Intervention.* New York: AFB, 2007. Print.

Smith, Millie, *SLK Routines Book, Using the Sensory Learning Kit, and SLK Guidebook and Assessment Forms, Using the Sensory Learning Kit.* Louisville: American Printing House for the Blind, 2005

Taylor, Jill Bolte Ph.D. *My Stroke of Insight.* Penguin Books Ltd., 2006. Print.

Websites

American Printing House for the Blind
Resources; Cortical Visual Impairment (CVI)
See especially the pull down menu under Resources
http://tech.aph.org/cvi/

Blind Babies Foundation
CVI Fact Sheet
http://blindbabies.org/learn/diagnoses-and-strategies/

CVI Society
Dr. Gordon Dutton
www.cvisociety.org

Facebook
Communities who focus on CVI:
https://www.facebook.com/cvicommunity?ref=hl
https://www.facebook.com/AdaptedWorld

Flashing Blinking Lights
Great website to order CVI friendly items like red blinking glasses, black gloves with lighted fingertips, light up pom poms and a red lighted tumbler
www.flashingblinkylights.com

LifeScience Technologies LLC
In conjunction with Dr. Roman, this company is working on developing a new (iPad) application that will allow teachers to build lesson plans according to a protocol developed by Dr. Roman. The CVI System has components available for monitoring, managing and improving a treatment program.
http://www.lifesciencetechnologies.com/Vision
https://www.youtube.com/watch?v=8cdN1eTW1Eo
Note; as of this printing, this application (The CVI System) was still in development

Dr. Lilli Nielsen
Dr. Lilli Nielsen's Books, videos and equipment
www.lilliworks.com

Little Bear Sees
Website raises awareness of CVI, offers resources and more. Two iPad Apps, specifically designed for students with CVI, are offered at this site.
http://www.littlebearsees.org/

Paths To Literacy
See especially the pull down menu under Resources and Strategies
www.pathstoliteracy.org

Perkins School for the Blind
Perkins offers a wide variety of resources, including Teaching Resources and Webinars. Appsolutely Engaging & Educational, Part 2 and Appsolutely Engaging and Educational are videos to watch on iPad Apps. There is a handout you can download.
www.perkins.org

Texas School for the Blind and Visually Impaired
This website includes a wealth of information and resources. See especially the section on *Communication for Children with Deafblindness, or Visual and Multiple Impairments* as well as *CVI Web Exercise* and *CVI Intervention*.
www.tsbvi.edu

The Jewish Guild for the Blind
Parent Tele Support Group for parents of children with CVI
Contact; Linda Gerra, EdD, Phone: 800-915-0306 E-mail: parent-groups@guildhealth.org
http://www.guildhealth.org/Programs-And-Services-Overview/Children-And-Vision/Parent-Tele-support

Vision Associates
Kathleen Appleby offers a CVI Checklist called, "Cortical Visual Impairment, Characteristics of Cortical Visual Impairment Checklist" which can be found at the Vision Kits website
http://visionkits.com/handouts

Wonderbaby
Wonderbaby.org is a project funded by Perkins School for the Blind to help parents of young children with visual impairments. They also offer a review of apps for children with visual impairments.
www.wonderbaby.org

Additional Web Sites and Articles That Offer Techniques and Strategies to Use with Students Who Have Cortical Visual Impairment

Burkhart, Linda J. "Developing Visual Skills for Children Who Face Cortical Visual Impairments." *Lindaburkhart.com*. Simplified Technology, n.d. Web. 22 Aug. 2016. <http://www.lindaburkhart.com/handcvi.htm>.

Demchak, MaryAnn, Charmaine Rickard, and Marty Elquist. "Tips for Home or School: Cortical Visual Impairment." *PDF; Cortical Visual Impairment - University of Nevada, Reno*. Nevada Dual Sensory Impairment Project, n.d. Web. 22 Aug. 2016. <http://unr.edu/ndsip/tipsheets/cvi.pdf>.

"Devising Strategies to Optimize Home and School Life for Children with Visual Impairment Due to Damage to the Brain." *Devising Strategies to Optimize Home and School Life for Children with Visual Impairment Due to Damage to the Brain*. Scottish Sensory Centre, 22 Jan. 2008. Web. 22 Aug. 2016. <http://www.ssc.education.ed.ac.uk/courses/VI&multi/vjan08iii.html>.

Dutton, Gordon. "Cerebral Visual Impairment in Children: A Practical Approach." *Emerald Education Systems*. Emerald Education Systems, n.d. Web. 22 Aug. 2016. <https://www.emeraldeducationsystems.com/course/ees/eescvi001>.

Edelman, Susan, Peggy Lashbrook, Annette Carey, Diane Kelly, Ruth Ann King, Christine Roman-Lantzy, and Cjogee Cloninger. "Cortical Visual Impairment: Guidelines and Educational Considerations." *Deaf-Blind Perspectives* 13 (2006): n. pag. *National Center on Deaf-Blindness*. Https://nationaldb.org/. Web. 22 Aug. 2016. <http://documents.nationaldb.org/dbp/pdf/may06.pdf>.

Gardier, Jeanne. "Strategies for Working with Children with Cortical Visual Impairment." Hand In Hand Project, n.d. Web. 22 Aug. 2016. <http://mtid.ri.umt.edu/MainMenu/Resources/FactSheets/StrategiesCorticalVisualImpairment.pdf>.

"Southern California CVI Consortium: CVI Packet." Low-Vision.org, n.d. Web. 22 Aug. 2016. <http://www.low-vision.org/wp-content/uploads/2012/10/Cortical-Visual-Impairment-Packet.pdf>.

Miscellaneous

CAD
Complexity at Distance Screening Tool
The CAD is a screening device used to observe if students have difficulty locating specific targets, at 10 feet, when presented on a typical Grade 2 or Grade 3 white board.
www.teacherspayteachers.com

Type in "CAD" in the search window.

So Smart Baby's Beginnings
DVD
So Smart Baby's Beginnings are a collection of children's DVDs with slow moving, single brightly colored targets. They are often entertaining for little ones with CVI. The collection has been discontinued but can still be purchased on Amazon.

My First Book of Symbols/My Second Book of Symbols
The book is designed to use with students who have a Cortical Visual Impairment (CVI). For anyone interested in obtaining a copy, contact Dr. Marva Gellhaus at the SDSBVI or by email at: marva.gellhaus@sdsbvi.northern.edu.

Texas School for the Blind and Visually Impaired
Training video through their outreach program.
http://www.tsbvi.edu/cvi-exercise

References

Alexander, Patricia K. "Cortical Visual Impairment." *Focus* 18.4 (n.d.): n. pag. *www.aph.org*. Web.

Anthony, Tanni L. "Cortical Visual Impairment: A Overview of Current Knowledge."*www.tsbvi.edu*. N.p., n.d. Web.

Baker-Nobles, Linda. "Cortical Visual Impairment." *Ski-Hi Institute News Exchange* Summer 1.3 (1996): n. pag. Print.

Baniel, Anat. *Kids beyond Limits: The Anat Baniel Method for Awakening the Brain and Transforming the Life of Your Child with Special Needs.* New York, NY: Perigee Trade, 2012.

Blaha, Robbie. *Calendars for Students with Multiple Impairments Including Deafblindness.* Austin, TX: Texas School for the Blind and Visually Impaired, 2001. Print.

Burkhart, Linda J. "Developing Visual Skills for Children Who Face Cortical Visual Impairments." *Simplified Technology*. Linda J. Burkhart, n.d. Web. 20 July 2016.

"Cortical Visual Impairment in Children." *Cortical Visual Impairment | Boston Children's Hospital*. Boston Children's Hospital, n.d. Web. 20 July 2016.

Daw, Nigel W. Visual Development. Boston (MA): Springer, 2006. Print.

Demchak, M., C. Pickard, and M. Elquist. "Tips for Home and School: Cortical Visual Impairment." (2011): n. pag. *Nevada Dual Sensory Impairment Project*. Web. <http://www.unr.edu/ndsip/secpagesEnglish/tips.html>.

Dennison, Elizabeth and Amanda Hall Lueck, *Proceedings of the Summit on Cerebral/Cortical Visual Impairment: Education, Family and Medical Perspectives:* April 30, 2005. New York: AFB, 2006. Print.

Dodson-Burk, Bonnie, and Christine Roman. *Preschool Orientation and Mobility Screening*. Alexandria, VA: Association for Education and Rehabilitation of the Blind and Visually Impaired, 2012. Print.

Doidge, Norman. *The Brain that Changes Itself: Stories of Personal Triumph from the Frontiers of Brain Science.* London: Penguin, 2008. Print.

Dutton, Gordon N. "Cerebral Visual Impairment: Working within and Around the Limitations of Vision." *Proceedings of the Summit on Cerebral/Cortical Visual Impairment*. New York, NY: AFB, 2005. 3-26. Print.

Dutton, Gordon N. "Cognitive Vision, Its Disorders and Differential Diagnosis in Adults and Children: Knowing Where and What Things Are." *Nature.com*. Nature Publishing Group, 2002. Web. 20 July 2016. <http://www.nature.com/eye/journal/v17/n3/full/6700344a.html>.

Dutton, G. and Martin Bax. *Visual Impairment in Children due to Damage to the Brain*. London: Mac Keith, 2010. Print.

Dutton, G. and Zihl, J. *Cerebral Visual Impairment in Children: Visuoperceptive and Visuocognitive Disorders*, Springer Verlag, 2014

Fogg, Laura. *Traveling Blind: Life Lessons from Unlikely Teachers*. Ukiah, CA: Medusa's Muse Pub., 2007. Print.

Good, William V. "Recent Advances in Cortical Visual Impairment." *Developmental Medicine and Child Neurology* 43.1 (January 2001): 56-60. Print.

Hoyt, C. S. "Visual Function in the Brain-damaged Child." *Nature.com*. Nature Publishing Group, 7 Aug. 2002. Web. 20 July 2016. <http://www.nature.com/eye/journal/v17/n3/full/6700364a.html>.

Jan, J. E., M. Groenveld, A. M. Sykanda, and C. S. Hoyt. "Behavioural Characteristics of Children with Permanent Cortical Visual Impairment." *Developmental Medicine and Child Neurology* (1987): 571-76. Print.

Kurson, Robert. *Crashing Through: A True Story of Risk, Adventure, and the Man Who Dared to See*. New York: Random House, 2007. Print.

Levak, Nancy, Gretchen Stone, and Virginia E. Bishop. "Programming for Students Who Have Severe Cortical Visual Impairments." *Low Vision: A Resource Guide with Adaptations for Students with Visual Impairments*. Austin, TX: Texas School for the Blind and Visually Impaired, 1994. 16-20. Print.

Lueck, Amanda Hall. *Functional Vision: A Practitioner's Guide to Evaluation and Intervention*. New York, NY: American Foundation for the Blind, 2004. Print.

Lueck, Amanda Hall, and Gordon Dutton, *Vision and the Brain: Understanding Cerebral Visual Impairment in Children*. New York; AFB, 2015. Print

Merzenich, Michael M. *Soft-wired: How the New Science of Brain Plasticity Can Change Your Life*. Parnassus Publishing, LLC, 2013. Print.

Morgan, Sam. "Neurological Visual Impairment - Also Known As: Cortical Visual Impairment, Delayed Visual Maturation, Cortical Blindness." *Texas School for the Blind and Visually Impaired*. Fact Sheet Reprinted with Permission from California Deafblind Services, n.d. Web. 20 July 2016. <http://www.tsbvi.edu/>.

Morse, Mary T. "Another View of Cortical Visual Impairment: Issues Related to Facial Recognition." *Proceedings of the Summit on Cerebral/Cortical Visual Impairment*. New York, NY: AFB, 2005. 131-35. Print.

Morse, Mary T. (1999). Cortical Visual Impairment: Some Words of Caution. RE:VIEW, 31 (1), 21-26

Nelson, Catherine, Van Dijk, J., Oster, T., & McDonnell, A. *Child-guided Strategies: The Van Dijk Approach to Assessment: For Understanding Children and Youth with Sensory Impairments and Multiple Disabilities.* Louisville, KY: American Printing House for the Blind, 2009. Print

Roman-Lantzy, Christine. *Cortical Visual Impairment: An Approach to Assessment and Intervention*. New York: AFB Press, 2007. Print

Sacks, Oliver W. *The Mind's Eye*. New York: Alfred A. Knopf, 2010. Print.

Shaman, Donna. "A Team Approach to Cortical Visual Impairment (CVI) in Schools." (n.d.): n. pag. May 2009. Web.

Smith, Millie, *SLK Routines Book, Using the Sensory Learning Kit, and SLK Guidebook and Assessment Forms, Using the Sensory Learning Kit.* Louisville, KY: American Printing House for the Blind, 2005. Guidebook.

Tallent Aubri, Fredy Bush, and Tallent, Andrei. *Little Bear Sees: How Children with Cortical Visual Impairment Can Learn to See*. Deadwood, OR: Little Bear Sees Publishing, 2012. Print.

Taylor, Jill Bolte Ph.D. *My Stroke of Insight*. Penguin Books Ltd., 2006. Print.

The Brain Fitness Program. Dr. Michael Merzenich. PBS, 2008. DVD

About the Author

Diane has over 30 years' experience in the area of Special Education. After receiving her Master's degree at San Francisco State University in Special Education - Visual Impairment, Diane started her career in Ventura County, California as a Certified Teacher of Students with Visual Impairments. Various positions over the years have taken her from California, to Oklahoma, New Mexico, Dubai UAE, Saudi Arabia, and Texas.

After Diane moved back to the States from Saudi Arabia in early 2002, she became interested in low vision as well as education of children with brain damage related vision loss. Diane decided at that time to go through ACVREP's program to attain certification as a Certified Low Vision Therapist.

During this time, the population of students with brain damage related vision loss was rising dramatically. Diane realized that more needed to be known about this special group of children and after taking numerous courses and researching this interesting area, she began tackling the challenge of better identification, assessment and intervention for students with Cortical Visual Impairment (CVI).

Diane currently conducts private evaluations and assessments for students who have a diagnosis of CVI. She also works closely with the Texas School for the Blind and Visually Impaired (TSBVI) on special projects related to CVI. Finally, she enjoys training other teachers and parents throughout the nation on strategies and interventions to use with students with Cerebral/Cortical Visual Impairment.

Diane lives in Sugar Land, Texas with her husband. She has one daughter, two sons, two daughters-in-law and one granddaughter, all who (lucky for her!) live nearby.

Made in the USA
Thornton, CO
04/04/25 01:18:15

f90603cf-6297-49d2-a6eb-917b1ed467dcR01